# NUMERACY

# TESTS

# HOW TO PASS NUMERACY TESTS

## SECOND EDITION

**HARRY TOLLEY and KEN THOMAS**

KOGAN
PAGE

First published in 1996
Reprinted 1997 (twice)
Reprinted 1998
Second edition 2000
Reprinted 2000
Reprinted 2001

Kogan Page Limited
120 Pentonville Road
London N1 9JN
UK

153.9324
423516
N153-9324

**British Library Cataloguing in Publication Data**

A CIP record for this book is available from the British Library.

ISBN 0 7494 3437 6

Typeset by Jean Cussons Typesetting, Diss, Norfolk
Printed and bound in Great Britain by Clays Ltd, St Ives plc

# Contents

# *Introduction*

Assessment in its different forms is an inescapable part of everyday life. We have all been subjected to assessment of the most obvious and formal kind when we have taken an examination, been interviewed for a job or taken a driving test. We are also engaged in the process of assessment whenever judgements are made about us (or when we evaluate other people) on the basis of, for example, appearance, speech and behaviour. However, the results of these assessments become more significant for us when the results have a direct effect on our livelihoods. This book is concerned with the testing of numeracy – one of the abilities that employers frequently assess for personnel selection purposes.

For many people selection tests present a serious obstacle to obtaining a job or, for those in employment, promotion to a more senior level. Many people fail to perform as well as they might on such tests because:

- they are nervous;
- they lack practice in test techniques;
- they are unfamiliar with the ways in which the questions are posed;
- through reliance on electronic calculators they may have become unaccustomed to doing even the most simple arithmetic calculations without them.

It is rare for candidates to be allowed to use calculators when taking selection tests. Consequently, your performance will be seriously impaired unless you have practised your basic number skills without the aid of a calculator, particularly under the time pressure you will be subjected to in a real test. Careful and systematic preparation for a selection test, including the use of the practice numeracy tests such as the ones provided here, can help you to overcome these causes of failure. It will also help you to avoid the sense of frustration that comes from knowing that you have not performed to the best of your ability.

The central purpose of this book, therefore, is to inform readers about selection tests in general and to offer guidance on how you might prepare yourself for taking them. Approximately two-thirds of the book is made up of practice tests of the type known as 'numeracy' or 'numerical reasoning' tests. These are commonly used for selection purposes in order to establish how competent candidates are in their ability to work with numbers. By working systematically through the tests you will become more familiar with the techniques required to complete them successfully, and this will help to build up your numeracy skills so that you feel more confident when taking an actual selection test. You will find the answers to the practice tests at the end of each chapter.

The practice tests in this book are similar to some of the numeracy tests most widely used by employers for selection purposes. They have arisen from a wide range of training and development work undertaken by the authors with major employers such as Civil Service departments and agencies and the police. The tests, therefore, have been piloted by real candidates taking tests such as the Police Initial Recruitment (PIR) Test, and the Executive Officer Qualifying Test (EOQT). Evaluation of the test results of these studies has demonstrated convincingly that regular use of these practice tests can significantly improve a candidate's performance, particularly when resitting a test that he/she has previously failed. Experience shows that doing well on a test is not only a matter of intelligence and aptitude, but also a matter of confidence and determination. If you lack confidence then you are unlikely to perform to the best of your ability on any test. Our evaluation studies have shown that regular use of practice tests helps to boost the candidates' confidence, and so enables them to cope more effectively with the nervousness and stress that everyone feels when taking an important test.

Use of the practice tests provided here, therefore, should help you to:

- become familiar with the different types of numerical reasoning tests that are commonly used for selection purposes;
- learn to work more effectively under the pressure of time experienced in real tests;
- improve your test techniques so that you do not lose marks through simple errors.

The continuous feedback you will receive as you work through the tests should help to boost your self-confidence. This in turn should help to reduce your anxiety, nervousness and any tendency to panic when confronted with real selection tests. However, in order to succeed you will need to be well motivated, to take practice seriously and to work hard on any weaknesses that become apparent in your results.

If you experience serious difficulty in coping with the practice tests given in the later chapters of this book it does not mean that you are a failure, and that you will never be able to succeed. What the practice tests will have done is to help you identify a learning need that you must address before you can make further progress. It is better to identify this weakness through practice tests than through the results of a selection test. If you find yourself in this situation you will probably need to build up your basic numeracy skills before you continue to work on the practice tests as part of your preparation for taking a selection test. Your local further education college or adult education centre may be able to help you overcome this difficulty. The likelihood is that they will have on offer a variety of courses in basic numeracy with flexible patterns of study and ways of working to suit a wide variety of circumstances including your own. Failing that, ask someone whom you know to have good number skills to act as your mentor and help you to overcome the weaknesses you have identified.

# A Brief Guide to Selection Tests

## Why do employers use selection tests?

In a highly competitive labour market many employers find that they receive very large numbers of applications for jobs whenever vacancies occur. In these circumstances it is essential that every effort is made to ensure that the right person is chosen for the job. Wrong selection decisions can lead to poor performance, low morale and high rates of staff turnover, all of which can prove to be very costly to an employer and stressful to an employee. As most selection tests can be taken in large groups they provide employers with a cost-effective means of choosing the most suitable people from large numbers of applicants. Those who achieve the test pass mark can then proceed to a second stage, which may well include interviews and/or assessments of performance in a variety of simulation exercises. Applicants for entry to the police service, for example, will first take the PIR Test and those who achieve the pass mark will then proceed to some form of extended assessment that may well include oral presentations, group decision-making exercises and formal interviews.

# What are selection tests?

Selection tests are specifically designed to measure how good people are at certain skills. The use of tests in personnel selection is based on the assumption that there are stable job-related individual differences between candidates, and that these differences can be measured with sufficient accuracy to be of use to employers in their selection and promotion procedures. Research shows that well-constructed psychometric tests predict job performance better than almost any other single selection measure. Appropriate tests produce more accurate results than other, more commonly used, selection measures such as interviews or references from other people. Tests give objective information about a candidate and have been shown to generally lead to better and fairer selection decisions.

# What is the difference between fair and unfair selection decisions?

Fairness in selection implies that applicants are chosen on the basis of aptitudes and abilities that can be shown to be relevant to a particular job and directly related to job performance. If selection decisions are not based on measures appropriate to the job, or the selection methods used are unreliable, then the selection may be unfair. The result might be that the most suitable candidates are rejected and the less suitable recruited or promoted.

Over the past 20 years the British government has introduced a number of measures intended to ensure greater equality in a number of aspects of social life. The Sex Discrimination Act (1975), the Race Relations Act (1976) and, in Northern Ireland, the Fair Employment (Northern Ireland) Acts (1976 and 1988) identify two types of discrimination, direct and indirect.

**Direct discrimination** involves treating someone less favourably on the basis of their ethnic origin, gender, marital status or, in Northern Ireland, religion.

**Indirect discrimination,** on the other hand, may often be unintended and can arise through the use of selection tests. It occurs, in this context, if an employer requires applicants to obtain a particular score on a selection test with which one group, defined, for example, by gender or race finds it difficult to comply. When a test has the effect of disproportionately excluding one gender, ethnic or racial group it is said to have an *adverse impact*. This is not unknown in test usage and differences in performance between males and females have been shown to occur from a relatively early age and continue into later life. For example, girls, as a group, significantly outperform boys on selection tests for entry into different kinds of secondary schools at the age of 11 years. Similarly, males, as a group, were shown to outperform females on certain elements of the EOQT that was used for entry to the Executive Officer grade in the Civil Service up to 1993. The reasons for these differences are extremely complex and include such things as differences in maturation rates, socio-economic backgrounds, learning opportunities and cultural and social attitudes. Nevertheless, in both of these instances individual test scores were, in the past, weighted to take account of the adverse impact of these tests.

# How is fairness achieved in test construction and administration?

There are two elements to test fairness – the tests themselves and the way in which the tests are used. Test constructors will make great efforts to ensure that tests are fair. Every selection test will be accompanied by a test manual in which the steps taken to ensure fairness will be described. These steps will generally include:

■ trialling with representative groups that include ethnic minorities;

■ checking for material that may be less familiar to some groups;

■ providing detailed and carefully worded instructions;

■ providing practice questions to help candidates become familiar with the test content and show what is expected of them;

■ ensuring that the test is free from obscure or ambiguous questions;

■ ensuring that the test provides a reliable measure of particular attributes that are relevant to the job;

■ providing normative data against which candidates can be properly compared.

When taking a test candidates will be provided with a standardised set of questions or problems that have to be answered in standardised conditions. The precise directions for the administration of a particular test will have been laid down by the test constructors in order that the test user can duplicate the administrative conditions with different groups of candidates. This is done in order to ensure that no group will have been advantaged or disadvantaged in terms of receiving the test instructions or in the way in which the test has been conducted. Although there may be slight variations, it is likely that most administrative conditions will have the following features.

■ Candidates will be seated comfortably, facing the administrator and reasonably spaced apart if there are a number of people taking the test at the same time.

■ Care will be taken to ensure that concentration will not be disturbed by telephone calls or visitors.

■ If the test is an observation-skills test based on video recordings, then the administrator will ensure that all candidates have an uninterrupted view of the screen.

■ Candidates will be provided with all the materials

necessary to complete the test, eg pencils, erasers, answer sheets and scrap paper.

■ The test session will begin with a brief introduction by the administrator. The administrator will explain the purpose of the test and tell candidates how the test is to be conducted. Many candidates will, naturally, feel nervous and the administrator will attempt to alleviate any undue anxieties in order that candidates perform at their best.

■ If the test requires candidates to provide gender and ethnic origin information then the administrator should explain that this is required for monitoring purposes only and not for use in the assessment of test results.

■ All instructions are carefully worded to ensure that candidates have all the information they need in order to complete the test correctly. The test administrator may read these instructions to the candidates and they may also be written in the test booklet. If this is the case you should follow them as they are being read by the test administrator. In some tests, candidates are left to read the instructions by themselves and this reading time may be included in the test time or additional time allocated for this purpose.

■ If time limits have been specified by the test constructor these will be strictly observed. This is essential in order to ensure that no group gains an advantage over another and, as a consequence, comparisons can be made between the performance of groups who take the test at different times.

■ Many tests provide example questions. In some tests candidates are asked to attempt these, while others have them already completed. One of the important features that the administrator will draw candidates' attention to will be the way in which answers are to be recorded. Many tests are in a multiple choice format

(A to E in the example given below) and candidates are required to record their answers by blocking out the appropriate small circle or box:

A            B            C            D            E

○            ○            ●            ○            ○

The purpose of the example questions is to ensure that candidates have a full understanding of what is required of them. If you use a tick or a cross, instead of a blacked out circle or square, your answer will be recorded as wrong even if the right choice has been made.

■ Candidates will generally then be given a final opportunity to ask questions about any of the test procedures before the administrator states clearly that the test has started.

■ The administrative instructions of some tests may not allow the administrator to give a warning that the end of the time allowed for the test is approaching.

## How are tests marked?

Marking is usually a straightforward, but very important part of testing. Obviously, it is essential that it is carried out correctly. Many tests will be objectively marked by the use of answer keys, on overlays, which are placed over the candidates' answer sheets. Before doing this the answer sheets will be checked for any irregularities. This could, for example, include the candidate blocking out more than one circle or box where only one was required. If this happens, the marker will cross through the answer in such a way as to ensure that it is marked 'wrong'.

Optical mark readers are used for the machine scoring of

certain types of answer sheets. Machine scoring is generally considered to give more reliable results than hand scoring and considerably increases the speed at which tests can be marked. This is very useful when large numbers of answer sheets have to be processed quickly.

If answer sheets are to be machine scored it is particularly important that the test instructions are followed precisely. All circles or squares must be adequately filled in according to the instructions provided or the optical marker will not detect them. In such an instance the item will be marked 'wrong'.

# What types of selection test might you be required to take?

A wide variety of tests is available to employers for selection purposes. The types that are most commonly used, together with the skills that they test, are described below.

## Logical reasoning

Tests of this type are intended to establish your ability to solve problems by thinking logically on the basis of the information provided. These tests are intended to select people for jobs where in the day-to-day activities of the workplace you will be required to think critically and solve problems as they arise.

## Numerical reasoning

These tests are intended to determine your ability to handle numbers. You may be required, for example, to answer questions based on data presented in a variety of forms including graphs and statistical tables. The level of difficulty of the problems will depend on the importance of numerical ability in the job to be undertaken. The tests are relevant to jobs where you will be required to work with numbers such as handling money, dealing with numbers as part of work in science and technology, and interpreting numerical data in the form of diagrams of sales and production figures.

## Verbal reasoning

These tests are intended to examine your ability to comprehend written information, and to understand and analyse the logic of written arguments. They are relevant to jobs where the understanding and evaluation of written information is an important skill. These are jobs where, for example, you might be required to read such things as reports and office circulars, memos from colleagues and letters from customers.

## Error checking

These tests are intended to examine your ability to check the accuracy of information that may be presented in a variety of forms. They are relevant to jobs where you might be required, for example, to check invoices against orders, data entered into a computer, or tables and accounts.

## Data interpretation

These tests are intended to examine your ability to interpret facts and figures presented in the form of statistical tables and diagrams. They are relevant to jobs in offices, shops, engineering and management where you might be required to make sense of information presented in these ways.

## Fault finding

These tests are intended to examine your ability to follow the logic of various circuits. They are relevant to occupations where you may be required to take a logical approach in order to find faults in technical systems. Electricians, car mechanics, electronic technicians and computer programmers are examples of jobs that require this skill.

## Spatial reasoning

These tests are intended to examine your ability to visualise objects or drawings when looked at from different directions. They are, for example, relevant to jobs in design, planning and engineering where you might be required to 'read' a plan and imagine how an object will look once it is finished.

# How to Prepare for Taking Selection Tests

The purpose of this chapter is to: help you to understand how practice can have a positive effect on your test results by helping you to perform to the best of your ability; give you guidance on how to use the practice tests and interpret your scores; and give you advice on the other things you can do to improve your numeracy skills.

## Can practice make a difference?

The value of practice to improve performance is well recognised in many areas. In the performing arts, for example, pianists, dancers, and singers are continually practising in order to maintain and further develop their skills. The value of practice in sport is perhaps best illustrated by a story that involves Gary Player who, at the time, was one of the world's leading golfers. In one particular tournament his ball finished in a sand bunker alongside the green. This made his next shot very difficult. Nevertheless, he played the ball out of the bunker to land about 18 inches from the hole. A spectator said, 'You were lucky there, Gary'. Gary Player replied, 'Yes, it's funny, I find the more I practise the luckier I get!'

The same is true of performance on selection tests. As we pointed out in the Introduction, many candidates underachieve in selection tests because they are over-anxious and because they do not know what to expect. The practice tests provided here are designed to help you to overcome both of these common causes of failure. The practice tests in the later chapters of this book will help you to become familiar with common examples of the type of tests known as 'numerical reasoning'. Regular practice will also give you the opportunity to work under conditions similar to those you will experience when taking real tests. In particular, you should become accustomed to working under the pressure of the strict time limits imposed in real test situations. Familiarity with the demands of the tests and working under simulated test conditions should help you to cope better with any nervousness you experience when taking tests that really matter. Strictly speaking, the old adage that 'practice makes perfect' may not apply to selection tests, but regular practice can make a difference – for the better!

## How to perform to the best of your ability on tests

Our experience over many years of preparing candidates for both selection tests and public examinations leads us to suggest that if you want to perform to the best of your ability on tests you should:

- make sure that you know what you have to do before you start – if you do not understand ask the test administrator;
- read the instructions carefully before the test starts in

order to make sure that you understand them – skim reading through them can cause you to overlook important details and make silly mistakes;

■   assume that the instructions (and the worked examples) are not the same as they were the last time you took the test – they may well have been changed, so read them as carefully as you can;

■   highlight or underline the 'command words' in the instructions, ie those words that tell you what you have to do;

■   work as quickly and accurately as you can once the test begins – every unanswered question is a scoring opportunity missed;

■   check frequently to make sure that the question you are answering matches the space you are filling in on the answer grid (as emphasised in Chapter 1);

■   avoid spending too much time on questions you find difficult – leave them and go back to them later if you have time;

■   enter your best reasoned choice if you are uncertain about an answer (but avoid simply guessing);

■   go back and check all your answers if you have any spare time after you have answered all the questions;

■   keep working as hard as you can throughout the test – the more correct answers you get the higher your score will be;

■   concentrate your mind on the test itself and nothing else – you cannot afford to allow yourself to be distracted;

■   be positive in your attitude – previous failures in tests and examinations should not be allowed to have a detrimental effect on your performance on this occasion; don't allow yourself to be 'beaten before you begin'!

# How to use the practice tests

To get the best out of the practice tests you should read and act on the advice given below. This consists of three sets of checklists to guide you through the different stages, ie **before** you begin, **during** the practice test and **after** you have completed it.

**Before** you begin to do any of the tests you should make sure that:

- you have the following: a supply of sharpened pencils, an eraser and some paper for doing any rough work;
- you have a clock or watch with an alarm that you can set to make sure that you work within the time limit you have set yourself;
- you are in a quiet room where you will not be disturbed or distracted and that has an uncluttered desk or table at which you can work;
- you have decided in advance which test you are going to tackle, and review what you learned from the previous practice session;
- you have read the instructions carefully on how to complete the test, even though you may think that you are already familiar with them;
- you have worked through the example(s) provided so that you know exactly what to do before you start.

You should then be ready to set your timer and turn your attention to the chosen practice test.

**During** the practice test you should try to:

- work quickly and systematically through the items – above all, do not panic;

- if you get stuck at any point move on to the next question as quickly as you can – you can always come back to any unfinished items at the end if you have time;
- remember to check over your answers if you have any spare time at the end;
- use spare paper for your rough work;
- stop working as soon as the time is up (and mark the point you have reached in the test if there are any items that you have not yet completed).

**After** the practice test you should:

- check your answers by referring to the answers given at the end of each chapter;
- put a (✓) against each question that you answered correctly and a (✗) next to each one you got wrong;
- add up the number of ticks to give you your score on the test as a whole;
- compare your score with those on previous tests of the same type to see what progress you are making;
- work through any items that you did not manage to complete in the test and check your answers;
- try to work out where you went wrong with any questions that you answered incorrectly.

If possible, talk through how you arrived at your answers with someone who has also done the test. Discussion of this kind can help to reinforce your learning by:

- helping you to understand why you got the wrong answer to certain questions;
- giving you a better understanding of the questions to which you got the right answers;
- suggesting alternative ways of arriving at the same answer to a question.

Discussion of this kind can help you to reach an understanding of the principles that underlie the construction of the test. In other words, you can begin to get 'inside the mind' of the person who set the questions. Working collaboratively with someone else can also help to keep you motivated and provide you with encouragement and 'moral' support if and when you need it.

# What do your practice test scores mean?

Because they tend to be shorter than real tests and have not been taken under the same conditions you should not read too much into your practice test scores. You will usually find that the real tests you sit are more exacting because they will be:

- longer than the examples provided in this book;
- administered formally in a standardised way (described in Chapter 1) by a person who has been trained in their use;
- more stressful than practice tests.

Nevertheless, your practice test scores should provide you with *feedback* on the following:

- how your performance on the same type of test (eg number sequences or data interpretation) varies from one practice test to another, and hence what progress you are making over time;
- how well you are doing on one type of test (eg number problems) compared to another (eg number sequences), and so what your strengths and weaknesses appear to be.

However, when trying to make sense of your practice test scores you should remember that:

- in real tests your score will be compared with the performance of a group of typical candidates to determine how well you have done;
- the pass mark in selection tests set by employers can go up or down depending on how many applicants there are and the number of job vacancies that are available at any one time;
- most tests are designed to ensure that very few candidates, if any, manage to get full marks;
- as a general rule, the typical score for the majority of candidates sitting real tests will be a little over a *half of the maximum* available, though this can vary from test to test.

## How to make the best use of feedback from practice tests

More important than your total score on a practice test is *how* you achieved that overall mark. For example, you could begin this diagnosis by making a note of the answer to the questions given below.

- How many questions did you attempt within the given time limit and how many remained unanswered?
- How many of the questions that you completed did you answer correctly?
- Where in the test were most of your incorrect answers (eg at the end when you were working in a hurry, or at the beginning when you may have been nervous or had not settled down properly)?

The answers to these questions should give you some pointers as to how you might *improve* your scores in future tests by changing your behaviour. For example:

- if you got most of the questions right, but left too many unanswered you should try to work more quickly next time;
- if you managed to answer all the questions, but got a lot of them wrong you should try to work more accurately, even though that might mean that you have to work more slowly.

Remember, the object of the exercise is to score as many correct answers as you can in the time allowed. Thus, there is a balance to be struck between speed and accuracy. Intelligent practice and careful evaluation of your results can help you to reach the right balance for you.

# Other things you can do to improve your numeracy skills

Numeracy tests seek to measure how effectively you can function with numbers. The computations involved in solving the numeracy problems included in such tests have to be done quickly and accurately. In order to do this you must be able to **add, subtract, multiply** and **divide**. Obvious though this may seem, the increased use of electronic calculators in schools and in the workplace has resulted in large numbers of people lacking confidence in their ability to perform these basic arithmetical functions either in their heads or on paper.

One of the most useful mathematical 'aids' that will help you to improve your performance on numeracy tests is a knowledge of **multiplication tables**. This should enable you to multiply and divide numbers quickly and accurately without the help of a calculator. If you do not know your tables already then our advice to you would be: learn them. One way of doing this is to construct a 'multiplication matrix' using the outline grid provided at the end of this chapter. Once completed you can refer to it whenever you need to check that you have got the right answer to a simple multiplication or division problem. However, as far as we are concerned, this is one instance where rote learning, reinforced by practice, can be very effective. Once you have a working knowledge of your tables you will be able to save a lot of time when taking selection tests – and be able to work much more accurately.

Regular practice of your basic arithmetic skills will help to improve your performance when taking numeracy tests and there are many opportunities in everyday life in which you can do this. For example, you can:

- calculate the cost of the contents of your shopping basket before you reach the checkout;
- use the exchange-rate tables in a daily newspaper to work out how many French francs or German marks you would receive for a given number of pounds sterling;
- use the tables given in the weather sections of a daily newspaper to calculate the difference in temperature between the world's warmest city and the world's coldest city, or the length of time between sunrise and sunset in London.

There are any number of basic numeracy problems that you could set yourself whenever you have an odd five or ten minutes to spare. It is important, however, to ensure that you are able to provide yourself with feedback to check on the accuracy of your calculations. For this reason it might be helpful if you carry a pocket calculator with you in order to check whether your answers to the problems you set yourself are right or wrong.

Some suggestions for particular aspects of numeracy to work

on are set out below in the form of a checklist. However, before you begin to put any of them into practice you should bear in mind the need to adopt a systematic approach to the development of your numeracy skills. You will not achieve the improvements you want to make by picking out areas at random from the checklist and trying them out spasmodically. Identify the areas in which you need to improve and then work consistently to a plan. Remember that regular practice and revision will help you to improve.

## Basic numeracy checklist

Try to ensure that you are competent in the following aspects of numeracy, all of which occur frequently in selection tests:

- weights and measures;
- units of time;
- adding, subtracting, multiplying and dividing of fractions;
- adding, subtracting, multiplying and dividing decimals;
- calculating the areas of shapes such as rectangles;
- calculating averages (eg speeds);
- calculating percentages;
- extracting information from line graphs, bar graphs, pie charts and statistical tables.

Since metric and non-metric measuring systems are common in everyday use (eg weights, money, linear distances) numeracy tests used for selection purposes usually include both. Hence you need to make yourself familiar with them and competent in their use.

It should be remembered that the benefits you are seeking to gain are cumulative – small improvements building on each other incrementally. It is more likely that such gains will be achieved by consistent application over a period of time measured in weeks and months rather than by a last ditch effort just before you take an important test. Preparing for tests and examinations is a bit like training for a race – it is the fitness that you build up over the long term that enables you to 'peak' at the right time.

## Multiplication matrix

Take a look at the 'multiplication matrix' below. Once completed this will give you the answer to any multiplication problem involving any two numbers up to and including the number 12. A quick look at the matrix shows that 2 × 7 = 14; 3 × 3 = 9; and 4 × 12 = 48. Now complete the matrix and then use it to help you to commit your multiplication tables to memory. When you have done that, add additional numbers to the matrix and learn them in the same way.

| 1 | 2 | 3 | 4 | 5 | 6 | 7 | 8 | 9 | 10 | 11 | 12 |
|---|---|---|---|---|---|---|---|---|----|----|----|
| 2 |   |   |   |   |   | 14 |   |   |    |    |    |
| 3 |   | 9 |   |   |   |   |   |   | 30 |    |    |
| 4 |   |   |   |   |   |   |   |   |    |    | 48 |
| 5 |   |   | 25 |   |   |   |   |   |    |    |    |
| 6 |   |   |   |   |   |   |   |   |    | 66 |    |
| 7 |   |   |   |   |   | 49 |   |   |    |    |    |
| 8 |   |   |   |   |   |   |   |   |    |    | 96 |
| 9 |   | 36 |   |   |   |   | 81 |   |    |    |    |
| 10 | 20 |   |   |   |   |   |   |   |    |    |    |
| 11 |   |   | 55 |   |   |   |   |   |    |    |    |
| 12 |   |   |   |   |   | 96 |   |   |    |    |    |

# 3

# *Taking Real Tests*

The aim of this chapter is to give you guidance on: what to do when taking real tests; and the different ways you might be expected to record your answers in such tests.

## What to do when taking real tests

**Before taking any tests,** for example, as part of the selection process for a job or for training, you should:

- find out as much as you can about the test in advance, eg ask if any examples are available of the types of question you will be asked;
- try to get a good night's sleep before the test;
- make sure that you get to the place where the test is to be held in good time so that you do not get anxious through having to rush;
- ensure that you have your glasses, contact lenses or hearing aid available if you need to use them during the test;
- inform the organisation or employer conducting the test in advance about any disability you may have so that they can make the necessary arrangements for you.

**At the test itself** you should:

- listen very carefully to the instructions you are given by the person administering the test;
- do exactly what you are told to do;
- read the written instructions carefully;
- work carefully through any practice questions that may be provided;
- make sure that you understand how you are required to record your answers;
- ask the administrator if there is anything that you do not understand;
- when told to begin the test read each question carefully before answering;
- work as quickly and accurately as you can;
- keep an eye on the time;
- stop working immediately when told to do so.

**After the test** you should:

- avoid worrying about your test results and get on with the rest of the selection process – people are usually selected by an employer for reasons other than high test scores;
- when it is appropriate to do so ask for feedback on your performance even if you are not offered the job or a place on the training scheme – it may help you to be successful the next time.

## How to record your answers

In the practice tests provided here you will find that the questions and the answer spaces are presented together. However, when you take real tests you will generally find that separate question and answer sheets or booklets will be used. This is because electronic scanners or optical mark readers (see Chapter 2) are often used to mark and score the test papers, especially with large organisations such as Civil Service departments and agencies.

It is essential, therefore, that your answers are presented in a form that the machine can understand. The instructions at the start of the test will usually inform you just exactly how to mark your answers, eg:

> Boxes must be marked with a dark pencil mark that completely fills the response position on the answer sheet. Light or partial marks □, ticks ☑, oblique strokes ▨ or crosses ☒ will be ignored and marked wrong.

Some questions will ask you to mark two or more circles/boxes instead of one, so read the question carefully, as an incorrect number of responses will also be marked wrong. If you make a mistake or change your mind, erase all unintentional marks completely from the answer grid with a rubber.

Many questions are presented in a multiple-choice format in which you are required to choose the correct answer from the given alternatives and to record this by putting a mark against the box or circle of your choice. For example, if you decide that the answer to a particular question was the one labelled B, you would record your answer like this:

A    ○        B    ●        C    ○        D    ○

If boxes were being used instead of circles and you decide that the answer to a particular question was the one labelled number 3, you would record your answer like this:

1    □        2    □        3    ■        D    □

Whichever system is used, you must take care to follow the instructions exactly – marks placed incorrectly will lead to your answer being marked as wrong.

# 4

# Number Problem Tests

In this type of multiple-choice test you are presented with a fairly simple problem and required to select the correct answer from five possible answers. Number problem tests are based on the four basic arithmetical operations (add, subtract, multiply and divide), simple fractions, decimals and percentages applied to quantities of money, objects, speed, time and area. Do not use a calculator. Use a sheet of paper or a note pad for any rough work.

The examples given below should help you to get the idea.

**Examples**

1. How much money would it cost to buy 7 loaves of bread at 52p a loaf?

   | A | B | C | D | E |
   |---|---|---|---|---|
   | £3.44 | £3.54 | £3.64 | £3.74 | £3.84 |

   > Answer = C

2. If I pay £4.56 for a tin of paint and 85p for a brush, how much will I have spent in total?

| A | B | C | D | E |
|---|---|---|---|---|
| £5.31 | £5.41 | £5.51 | £5.61 | £5.71 |

Answer = B

Four practice tests of this type are given below. Each test consists of 20 questions for which you should allow yourself 8 minutes per test. Work as quickly and as accurately as you can. If you are not sure of an answer, mark your best choice, but avoid wild guessing. If you want to change an answer, rub it out completely and then write your new answer in the space provided. Give yourself one mark for each correct answer and make a note of the scores to see if you are improving from one test to another.

# Number problems

## Test 1

1. Two out of every 8 cyclists are questioned in a spot-check. Out of 408 cyclists, how many are questioned?

| A | B | C | D | E |
|---|---|---|---|---|
| 102 | 100 | 88 | 80 | 40 |

Answer =

2. If I pay £4.40 for lunch and £2.75 for tea, how much in total have I spent?

| A | B | C | D | E |
|---|---|---|---|---|
| £6.95 | £7.05 | £7.15 | £7.25 | £7.35 |

Answer =

3.  A worker's shift begins at 05.30 and lasts for 9 hours. What time does it end?

    | A | B | C | D | E |
    |---|---|---|---|---|
    | 15.30 | 15.00 | 14.30 | 14.00 | 13.30 |

    Answer =

4.  How much would it cost to buy 3 bicycle lights at £3.50 each?

    | A | B | C | D | E |
    |---|---|---|---|---|
    | £9.50 | £11.50 | £12.00 | £11.00 | £10.50 |

    Answer =

5.  If I pay 23p for a bus ticket, £2.35 for a train ticket and £10.40 for a taxi fare, how much have I spent in total?

    | A | B | C | D | E |
    |---|---|---|---|---|
    | £2.98 | £5.75 | £9.98 | £10.63 | £12.98 |

    Answer =

6.  If my bus journey takes 35 minutes and my train journey takes 55 minutes, how long is my journey in total?

    | A | B | C | D | E |
    |---|---|---|---|---|
    | 1½ hours | 1¼ hours | 70 minutes | ¾ hour | 85 minutes |

    Answer =

7.  I leave my house at 06.00 and return at 14.15. How many hours have I been out of my house?

    | A | B | C | D | E |
    |---|---|---|---|---|
    | 20½ | 18¾ | 8¼ | 6 | 2¼ |

    Answer =

8. If 5 cars fill up their tanks with 120 litres of diesel each, how many litres of diesel are used in total?

| A | B | C | D | E |
|---|---|---|---|---|
| 6,000 | 600 | 500 | 460 | 240 |

Answer =

9. A car park holds 550 cars when it is full. How many cars does it hold when it is half full?

| A | B | C | D | E |
|---|---|---|---|---|
| 1,100 | 250 | 55 | 275 | 350 |

Answer =

10. In a car park of 660 cars, 20 per cent are yellow cars. How many yellow cars are in the car park?

| A | B | C | D | E |
|---|---|---|---|---|
| 680 | 230 | 330 | 132 | 33 |

Answer =

11. If a machinist earns £110 a week, how much will she earn in 12 weeks?

| A | B | C | D | E |
|---|---|---|---|---|
| £12,000 | £1,210 | £1,320 | £1,120 | £122 |

Answer =

12. A motorist is travelling at 72.5 mph in an area where the speed limit is 50 mph. By how much is the driver exceeding the speed limit?

| A | B | C | D | E |
|---|---|---|---|---|
| 20.5 mph | 22.5 mph | 52.5 mph | 70.5 mph | 120.5 mph |

Answer =

13. If a police officer is asked for directions on average 3 times a day, how many directions in total will she give in 7 days?

| A | B | C | D | E |
|---|---|---|---|---|
| 4 | 10 | 17 | 21 | 27 |

Answer =

14. Out of 13,750 people in a football stadium, 10 per cent are season ticket holders. How many people do not have a season ticket?

| A | B | C | D | E |
|---|---|---|---|---|
| 1,375 | 1,775 | 10,750 | 12,375 | 15,125 |

Answer =

15. If I ran 18 miles in 3 hours, what is my average speed?

| A | B | C | D | E |
|---|---|---|---|---|
| 21 mph | 13 mph | 8 mph | 6 mph | 3 mph |

Answer =

16. My shift is 9 hours long. If I begin work at 13.30, what time do I finish work?

| A | B | C | D | E |
|---|---|---|---|---|
| 04.30 | 09.30 | 19.30 | 21.00 | 22.30 |

Answer =

17. Each roll of wallpaper is 1 metre wide. How many widths of wallpaper are needed to paper a wall 12,500 cm long?

| A | B | C | D | E |
|---|---|---|---|---|
| 12,500 | 125 | 25 | 12.5 | 2 .5 |

Answer =

18. Each tile is 2 metres × 2 metres. How many tiles are needed to cover a floor 40 metres × 40 metres?

| A | B | C | D | E |
|---|---|---|---|---|
| 440 | 400 | 200 | 40 | 20 |

Answer =

19. How much would it cost to buy 7 envelopes at 23p each?

| A | B | C | D | E |
|---|---|---|---|---|
| 73p | £1.41 | £1.61 | £1.81 | £2.10 |

Answer =

20. A crate of milk contains 8 bottles and costs £4.00. How much do 3 bottles of milk cost?

| A | B | C | D | E |
|---|---|---|---|---|
| £2.40 | £1.48 | £1.24 | £1.50 | £2.50 |

Answer =

# Test 2

1. I began the day with £10.00 in my pocket. By the evening I had £2.73 left. How much had I spent?

| A | B | C | D | E |
|---|---|---|---|---|
| £10.73 | £8.73 | £7.27 | £6.27 | £2.73 |

Answer =

2. My shift starts at 06.30 and ends at 14.30. How many hours will I have worked if I work for 7 days?

| A | B | C | D | E |
|---|---|---|---|---|
| 56 | 48 | 46 | 38 | 36 |

Answer =

3.  I earn £110 per week. I have been given a 5 per cent pay rise. What will my new weekly wage be?

| A | B | C | D | E |
|---|---|---|---|---|
| £125.00 | £115.50 | £115.00 | £110.50 | £105.00 |

Answer =

4.  What percentage of £32.00 is £8.00?

| A | B | C | D | E |
|---|---|---|---|---|
| 8% | 20% | 23% | 25% | 32% |

Answer =

5.  If two pairs of boots cost £46.00, how much would one pair cost?

| A | B | C | D | E |
|---|---|---|---|---|
| £10.50 | £11.50 | £13.00 | £23.00 | £26.00 |

Answer =

6.  The police station is 1,180 metres from the library. The supermarket is half way between the police station and the library. How many metres is the supermarket from the library?

| A | B | C | D | E |
|---|---|---|---|---|
| 2,360 | 1,200 | 590 | 600 | 1,800 |

Answer =

7.  If I drive at 30 mph, how long (in hours) will it take me to drive 90 miles?

| A | B | C | D | E |
|---|---|---|---|---|
| ½ | 3 | 6 | 9 | 12 |

Answer =

8. How many square metres of turf will I need to cover two areas of ground, one of which is 7 metres × 3 metres and the other 4.5 metres × 2.5 metres?

| A | B | C | D | E |
|---|---|---|---|---|
| 31.5 | 31.75 | 32 | 32.25 | 32.5 |

Answer =

9. If I drive 200 miles, how many hours will the journey take if I drive 40 mph for 100 miles and 80 mph for 100 miles?

| A | B | C | D | E |
|---|---|---|---|---|
| 3¾ | 4¾ | 5 | 3½ | 3 |

Answer =

10. If 9 out of 10 cars use unleaded petrol, what percentage of cars use leaded petrol?

| A | B | C | D | E |
|---|---|---|---|---|
| 90% | 80% | 81% | 10% | 9% |

Answer =

11. If the house subsides at a rate of 2 cm per year, how many years will it be before it has subsided half a metre?

| A | B | C | D | E |
|---|---|---|---|---|
| 500 | 50 | 25 | 12½ | ½ |

Answer =

12. The blue car costs £3,500, the red car costs £6,700 and the green car costs £7,800. What is the average price of these 3 cars?

| A | B | C | D | E |
|---|---|---|---|---|
| £18,000 | £12,500 | £9,000 | £6,000 | £3,000 |

Answer =

13. A book of stamps used to cost £1.00, now it costs £1.20. By what percentage has the price increased?

| A | B | C | D | E |
|------|------|-----|-----|----|
| 120% | 100% | 20% | 12% | 5% |

Answer =

14. Bob is 29 years old, Peter is 27 years old and Sally is 33 years old. What is the total (in years) of all their ages?

| A | B | C | D | E |
|----|----|----|----|----|
| 79 | 83 | 89 | 90 | 97 |

Answer =

15. If you walk along a straight stretch of road from the post office past the hospital to the bus station, how far will you have walked in metres if the post office is 120 metres from the hospital, and the hospital is 189 metres from the bus station?

| A | B | C | D | E |
|-----|-----|-----|-----|----|
| 389 | 309 | 299 | 189 | 69 |

Answer =

16. A bus carrying 26 passengers arrives 8 minutes late at the factory. How many minutes of work is lost in total by the 26 passengers?

| A | B | C | D | E |
|-----|-----|-----|-----|---|
| 340 | 308 | 268 | 208 | 8 |

Answer =

17. Each car holds 220 litres of petrol. How many cars will a 2,420-litre tank fill?

| A | B | C | D | E |
|---|---|---|---|---|
| 10 | 11 | 12 | 22 | 100 |

Answer =

18. What percentage of £8.00 is 20p?

| A | B | C | D | E |
|---|---|---|---|---|
| 16% | 10% | 8% | 2.5% | 2% |

Answer =

19. There are 75 police officers at a football match. If one-third of the officers are inside the ground and the rest are outside, how many are outside the ground?

| A | B | C | D | E |
|---|---|---|---|---|
| 100 | 50 | 33 | 25 | 12 |

Answer =

20. A nurse works for two-thirds of a 24-hour day. How many hours does he work in 5 days?

| A | B | C | D | E |
|---|---|---|---|---|
| 120 | 96 | 80 | 48 | 24 |

Answer =

# Test 3

1.  If 1 litre of paint covers an area of 60 metres × 10 metres,
    how many litres of paint are needed to cover a wall 30
    metres × 5 metres?

    | A | B | C | D | E |
    |---|---|---|---|---|
    | 6 | 2 | 0.5 | 0.25 | 0.33 |

    Answer =

2.  If I have £7.37 in my pocket, and spend £3.43 and have
    £1.52 left in my pocket, how much money must I have
    lost?

    | A | B | C | D | E |
    |---|---|---|---|---|
    | £12.32 | £4.95 | £3.94 | £2.42 | £1.52 |

    Answer =

3.  How many complete lengths of rope, each 4.7 metres long,
    can be cut from a rope 92 metres long?

    | A | B | C | D | E |
    |---|---|---|---|---|
    | 21 | 20 | 19 | 16 | 11 |

    Answer =

4.  If someone earning £140 a week receives a pay increase of
    2.5 per cent, by how much will the pay increase?

    | A | B | C | D | E |
    |---|---|---|---|---|
    | £2.00 | £2.50 | £3.00 | £3.50 | £4.00 |

    Answer =

5.  If it takes me 20 minutes to water a garden that is 25 square metres, how many minutes will it take me to water a garden that is 50 metres × 2.5 metres?

| A | B | C | D | E |
|---|---|---|---|---|
| 120 | 100 | 80 | 60 | 40 |

Answer =

6.  On 4 consecutive days I work the following hours: 06.00 to 14.00; 07.30 to 18.00; 07.00 to 13.00; and 08.30 to 19.30. How many hours am I not working over those 4 days?

| A | B | C | D | E |
|---|---|---|---|---|
| 96 | 60½ | 60 | 38½ | 35½ |

Answer =

7.  What is the average height of the 5 people whose heights are 2.01 m, 1.92 m, 1.57 m, 1.88 m, 2.05 m?

| A | B | C | D | E |
|---|---|---|---|---|
| 188.6 cm | 180 cm | 18.9 cm | 1.89 cm | 1.88 cm |

Answer =

8.  If prices rise by 8 per cent, what would be the new price of an item now costing £160.00?

| A | B | C | D | E |
|---|---|---|---|---|
| £172.80 | £170.00 | £168.00 | £166.00 | £162.80 |

Answer =

9.  How many 7 cm × 7 cm tiles are needed to cover a surface that measures 84 cm × 84 cm?

| A | B | C | D | E |
|---|---|---|---|---|
| 164 | 144 | 124 | 120 | 84 |

Answer =

10. The speed limit in an area is 40 mph. If I were travelling at 67.5 mph, by how much would I have to reduce my speed so that I was travelling at the speed limit?

| A | B | C | D | E |
|---|---|---|---|---|
| 40 mph | 33.5 mph | 30 mph | 27.5 mph | 23.5 mph |

Answer =

11. If I paid 5 parking fines of £12.00 each, how much have I paid in total?

| A | B | C | D | E |
|---|---|---|---|---|
| £62.00 | £60.00 | £52.00 | £50.00 | £48.00 |

Answer =

12. Seven 57-seat buses are booked to carry a football supporters' club to a match. How many supporters can travel on the buses?

| A | B | C | D | E |
|---|---|---|---|---|
| 399 | 449 | 499 | 549 | 599 |

Answer =

13. Four safes, each containing £352.00, have been stolen. How much money has been stolen altogether?

| A | B | C | D | E |
|---|---|---|---|---|
| £1,652.00 | £1,408.00 | £1,208.00 | £1052.00 | £888.00 |

Answer =

14. It takes me 7 hours to travel 420 miles. What is my average speed?

| A | B | C | D | E |
|---|---|---|---|---|
| 70 mph | 62 mph | 60 mph | 40 mph | 35 mph |

Answer =

15. If a shopper has £37.00 and spends £21.32, how much change will she have?

| A | B | C | D | E |
|---|---|---|---|---|
| £19.32 | £18.58 | £17.68 | £16.58 | £15.68 |

Answer =

16. A survey samples 1 out of every 9 households. Out of 117 households, how many would be sampled?

| A | B | C | D | E |
|---|---|---|---|---|
| 10 | 11 | 12 | 13 | 14 |

Answer =

17. The average weekly wage is £213.00. If I only earn one-third of this, how much do I earn?

| A | B | C | D | E |
|---|---|---|---|---|
| £71.00 | £69.00 | £142.00 | £141.00 | £73.00 |

Answer =

18. The number of arrests has risen by 6 per cent this year. What is the total number of arrests this year, if 500 arrests were made last year?

| A | B | C | D | E |
|---|---|---|---|---|
| 800 | 630 | 530 | 506 | 30 |

Answer =

19. If I work 18 out of 24 hours, what percentage of the day have I worked?

| A | B | C | D | E |
|---|---|---|---|---|
| 25 | 35 | 50 | 65 | 75 |

Answer =

20. A person spends 40 per cent of his weekly wage on clothes. He earns £230.00 a week. In 2 weeks how much has he spent on clothes?

| A | B | C | D | E |
|---|---|---|---|---|
| £92 | £102 | £115 | £164 | £184 |

Answer =

## Test 4

1.  A roll of wire is 100 metres long. How many rolls are needed to surround a square park that measures 500 metres × 500 metres?

| A | B | C | D | E |
|---|---|---|---|---|
| 2,500 | 200 | 20 | 10 | 5 |

Answer =

2.  My garden is 13 metres square of which half is paved. How many square metres are unpaved?

| A | B | C | D | E |
|---|---|---|---|---|
| 169 | 139 | 84.5 | 42.25 | 6.5 |

Answer =

3. Four streets have the following number of houses on them: 18; 23; 41; 37. What is the average number of houses per street?

| A | B | C | D | E |
|---|---|---|---|---|
| 29.75 | 31.75 | 33 | 37.5 | 119 |

Answer =

4. The ages of a group of people are: 29; 47; 53; 17; 48; 59; 22; and 33. What percentage are over 40 years of age?

| A | B | C | D | E |
|---|---|---|---|---|
| 60% | 50% | 40% | 10% | 4% |

Answer =

5. I had £12.43 and spent £7.67. How much did I have left?

| A | B | C | D | E |
|---|---|---|---|---|
| £5.67 | £5.03 | £4.83 | £4.76 | £3.64 |

Answer =

6. I was caught speeding in a 50 mph area. I was travelling 23 mph above the speed limit. How fast was I travelling?

| A | B | C | D | E |
|---|---|---|---|---|
| 83 mph | 73 mph | 67 mph | 63 mph | 27 mph |

Answer =

7. Six people share the £14.46 taxi fare. How much does each person pay?

| A | B | C | D | E |
|---|---|---|---|---|
| £4.12 | £3.61 | £2.81 | £2.61 | £2.41 |

Answer =

8. How many 15-litre drums are needed to fill a 450-litre petrol tank?

| A | B | C | D | E |
|----|----|----|----|----|
| 30 | 25 | 15 | 5 | 3 |

Answer =

9. There is an average of 5 accidents an hour. How many accidents would you expect in one full day?

| A | B | C | D | E |
|----|-----|-----|-----|-----|
| 96 | 112 | 120 | 125 | 150 |

Answer =

10. A fitter's shift begins at 04.30 and ends at 13.15. How many hours has he worked?

| A | B | C | D | E |
|-----|-----|----|-----|-----|
| 8¾ | 9¼ | 8 | 7¾ | 7¼ |

Answer =

11. What is the average speed of 5 cars travelling at the following speeds: 60 mph, 75 mph, 25 mph, 40 mph, 50 mph?

| A | B | C | D | E |
|--------|--------|--------|--------|--------|
| 45 mph | 50 mph | 55 mph | 60 mph | 65 mph |

Answer =

12. 75 per cent of the spectators in a stadium that holds 1,244 people are under cover. How many spectators are not under cover when the stadium is full?

| A | B | C | D | E |
|---|---|---|---|---|
| 1,033 | 933 | 811 | 411 | 311 |

Answer =

13. A cyclist travels at 9 mph. How many hours will he take to cycle 67.5 miles?

| A | B | C | D | E |
|---|---|---|---|---|
| 5½ | 6½ | 7 | 7½ | 8 |

Answer =

14. A shopper spends £29.99 on shoes, £23.50 on trousers and £18.00 on a shirt. How much will he have left if he started with £120?

| A | B | C | D | E |
|---|---|---|---|---|
| £61.49 | £58.51 | £51.49 | £48.51 | £41.49 |

Answer =

15. A shop reduces all of its prices by 12.5 per cent. What is the sale price of an easy chair that originally cost £160?

| A | B | C | D | E |
|---|---|---|---|---|
| £145 | £140 | £135 | £130 | £125 |

Answer =

16. A garage charges £45 for parts and £105 for labour. How much is the total bill when VAT at 17.5 per cent is added?

| A | B | C | D | E |
|---|---|---|---|---|
| £156.25 | £166.25 | £176.25 | £186.25 | £196.25 |

Answer =

17. How many fencing panels will I need to enclose a garden that is 24 metres long and 9 metres wide if the panels are 3 metres long × 2 metres high?

| A | B | C | D | E |
|---|---|---|---|---|
| 11 | 22 | 26 | 30 | 33 |

Answer =

18. A betting syndicate of five people wins £140. What was the total profit if they each staked £2.50?

| A | B | C | D | E |
|---|---|---|---|---|
| £137.50 | £135.00 | £132.50 | £130.00 | £127.50 |

Answer =

19. In one week a mechanic worked 35 hours at normal time and 6 hours overtime at double the rate for normal time. How much did he earn if the normal time rate of pay is £6.00 an hour?

| A | B | C | D | E |
|---|---|---|---|---|
| £252 | £262 | £272 | £282 | £292 |

Answer =

20. How many miles will a lorry have travelled if it maintained an average speed of 35 mph for 6½ hours?

| A | B | C | D | E |
|---|---|---|---|---|
| 220 | 222.5 | 225 | 227.5 | 230 |

Answer =

# Number problem tests: answers

## Test 1

| | | | | | | | |
|---|---|---|---|---|---|---|---|
| 1. | A | 6. | A | 11. | C | 16. | E |
| 2. | C | 7. | C | 12. | B | 17. | B |
| 3. | C | 8. | B | 13. | D | 18. | B |
| 4. | E | 9. | D | 14. | D | 19. | C |
| 5. | E | 10. | D | 15. | D | 20. | D |

## Test 2

| | | | | | | | |
|---|---|---|---|---|---|---|---|
| 1. | C | 6. | C | 11. | C | 16. | D |
| 2. | A | 7. | B | 12. | D | 17. | B |
| 3. | B | 8. | D | 13. | C | 18. | D |
| 4. | D | 9. | A | 14. | C | 19. | B |
| 5. | D | 10. | D | 15. | B | 20. | C |

## Test 3

| | | | | | | | |
|---|---|---|---|---|---|---|---|
| 1. | D | 6. | B | 11. | B | 16. | D |
| 2. | D | 7. | A | 12. | A | 17. | A |
| 3. | C | 8. | A | 13. | B | 18. | C |
| 4. | D | 9. | B | 14. | C | 19. | E |
| 5. | B | 10. | D | 15. | E | 20. | E |

## Test 4

| | | | | | | | |
|---|---|---|---|---|---|---|---|
| 1. | C | 6. | B | 11. | B | 16. | C |
| 2. | C | 7. | E | 12. | E | 17. | B |
| 3. | A | 8. | A | 13. | D | 18. | E |
| 4. | B | 9. | C | 14. | D | 19. | D |
| 5. | D | 10. | A | 15. | B | 20. | D |

# *Data Interpretation Tests (1)*

The data interpretation tests provided here are similar to the multiple-choice tests commonly used in personnel selection. There are four practice tests, each consisting of 15 questions. You should allow yourself 20 minutes to complete each test. Your aim should be to work as quickly and as accurately as you can, attempting as many questions as possible in the time allowed.

Each test consists of a series of statistical tables followed by questions related to each table. For each question there are five possible answers. Your task is to work out which is the correct answer to each question, using the data presented on the relevant table, and then record this in the space provided.

**Example**

Price of fuel for heating in pence per useful kilowatt hour.

| Fuel | Pence |
|------|-------|
| Butane (room heater) | 4.6 |
| Electricity (fan heater) | 5.2 |
| Kerosene (central heating) | 2.9 |
| Gas (wall heater) | 1.7 |
| Coal (open fire) | 3.5 |
| Anthracite (central heating) | 2.2 |

1.  Which heating fuel is approximately twice the price of gas?

    Butane    Electricity    Kerosene    Coal    Anthracite

    > Answer = Coal

# Data interpretation

## Test 1

The following table shows the number of emergencies attended by 6 fire brigade sub-stations during a 5-month period:

| Sub-station | May | June | July | Aug | Sept |
|---|---|---|---|---|---|
| A | 11 | 10 | 12 | 26 | 27 |
| B | 22 | 23 | 20 | 42 | 28 |
| C | 36 | 46 | 58 | 68 | 43 |
| D | 21 | 22 | 24 | 27 | 26 |
| E | 16 | 16 | 15 | 19 | 12 |
| F | 24 | 18 | 26 | 37 | 29 |

1.  What was the total number of emergencies attended by all 6 sub-stations in June and July?

    283            309            290            310            287

    Answer =

2.  Which of the following sub-stations had the biggest increase in the number of emergencies attended in August compared to July?

    A            B            C            D            E

    Answer =

3.   If sub-station C had attended only half the number of emergencies over the 5-month period, which of the following sub-stations would have attended most emergencies?

A            B            C            D            E

Answer =

Polls of the voting intentions of a sample of the population were carried out over a period of 6 months and the percentage support for the different political parties was as follows:

|         |    |    | Party |    |    |
|---------|----|----|-------|----|----|
| Month   | A  | B  | C     | D  | E  |
| Jan     | 18 | 20 | 24    | 17 | 21 |
| Feb     | 18 | 22 | 22    | 18 | 20 |
| Mar     | 19 | 23 | 21    | 20 | 17 |
| April   | 22 | 23 | 21    | 21 | 13 |
| May     | 23 | 24 | 18    | 20 | 15 |
| June    | 24 | 25 | 18    | 17 | 16 |

4.   In which month was there the greatest difference between the party gaining the most support and the party gaining the least support?

Jan            Feb            Mar            April            May

Answer =

5.   Which 2 parties received the same level of support over the 6-month period?

A and B      D and E      C and E      A and C      B and D

Answer =

6.  If Party A received only half of the support given to it in June and instead the support was distributed among Parties C, D and E, with Party E benefiting by twice as much as each of the other two, which two parties would have received the greatest amount of support in the month of June?

B and C    D and E    C and E    B and D    B and E

Answer =

Five shops averaged the following monthly sales of sports goods in one calendar year:

|         |    | Shops |    |    |    |
|---------|----|----|----|----|----|
| Items   | A  | B  | C  | D  | E  |
| Footballs | 30 | 14 | 24 | 30 | 20 |
| Shorts  | 29 | 24 | 24 | 34 | 32 |
| Shirts  | 20 | 30 | 32 | 34 | 16 |
| Boots   | 30 | 44 | 40 | 22 | 18 |
| Trainers | 40 | 22 | 36 | 21 | 26 |
| Tracksuits | 20 | 24 | 24 | 28 | 14 |

7.  Which 2 shops sold the same total number of items?

A and B    C and D    B and C    D and E    A and D

Answer =

8.  If each sales assistant in shop C sold 24 items, with the exception of one who sold 36 items, how many sales assistants are there in shop C?

6         7         8         9         10

Answer =

9. If the staff of shop C had sold only half the number of items they did, and shops A and D had sold no tracksuits, which shop would have sold the most items?

A          B          C          D          E

Answer =

The sources of income of 5 British universities in 1 year were as follows:

|  | University | | | | |
|---|---|---|---|---|---|
| Source | A | B | C | D | E |
|  | % | % | % | % | % |
| Public funds | 48 | 46 | 54 | 46 | 58 |
| Research contracts | 21 | 16 | 20 | 19 | 16 |
| Investments | 16 | 10 | 12 | 19 | 10 |
| Conferences | 8 | 14 | 9 | 6 | 5 |
| Vacation lettings | 4 | 8 | 3 | 7 | 6 |
| Donations | 3 | 6 | 2 | 3 | 5 |

10. Which 2 universities received the same proportion of their income from combined public funds and research contracts sources?

A and B    C and D    B and C    D and E    C and E

Answer =

11. Which university received the greatest proportion of its total income from research contracts, investments and vacation lettings combined?

A          B          C          D          E

Answer =

12. Which university received the smallest proportion of its total income from investments and donations combined?

A          B          C          D          E

Answer =

The percentage unemployment rates in 5 countries, over a 5-year period, were as follows:

| Country | 1986 | 1987 | Year 1988 | 1989 | 1990 |
|---------|------|------|------|------|------|
| A | 4.2 | 4.6 | 4.9 | 5.3 | 5.5 |
| B | 4.4 | 4.5 | 4.4 | 4.3 | 4.6 |
| C | 4.9 | 5.1 | 5.3 | 5.6 | 5.0 |
| D | 8.7 | 9.0 | 9.2 | 9.4 | 9.0 |
| E | 5.4 | 5.9 | 5.9 | 6.3 | 6.8 |
| F | 6.8 | 7.0 | 7.2 | 7.5 | 8.1 |

13. In which 2 countries was there the same percentage increase in unemployment in 1990 compared to 1986?

A and B     A and F     B and C     D and E     B and E

Answer =

14. What was the average percentage change in unemployment across all 6 countries in 1990 compared to 1989?

  – 0.2          – 0.1          +0.1          +0.2          +0.3

Answer =

15. What was the difference in the unemployment rate, averaged over the 5-year period, in country D compared to country E?

+1              +2              +3              +4              +5

Answer =

# Test 2

The percentage of households owning durable items in 5 regions were:

|                 |    | Region |    |    |    |
| Item            | A  | B  | C  | D  | E  |
| --------------- | -- | -- | -- | -- | -- |
| Microwave       | 48 | 41 | 49 | 46 | 43 |
| Fridge          | 63 | 61 | 69 | 60 | 64 |
| Dishwasher      | 11 | 7  | 11 | 10 | 8  |
| Washing machine | 82 | 85 | 87 | 83 | 80 |
| Freezer         | 41 | 33 | 45 | 42 | 44 |
| Tumble dryer    | 32 | 33 | 27 | 28 | 26 |

1. Which region had the highest percentage of households not owning a microwave?

A            B            C            D            E

Answer =

2. If a further 4 per cent of households in each of regions A and B owned dishwashers together with a further 5 per cent in region C, what would be the average percentage of households owning dishwashers across all 5 regions?

9              10              11              12              13

Answer =

Selected crime statistics in the first quarter of one year in 5 divisions of one police force are shown in the following table:

| Incidents | Divisions | | | | |
|---|---|---|---|---|---|
| | A | B | C | D | E |
| Robbery | 68 | 99 | 52 | 52 | 62 |
| Wounding | 26 | 27 | 14 | 29 | 24 |
| Theft | 30 | 84 | 31 | 27 | 29 |
| Arson | 31 | 38 | 30 | 30 | 26 |
| Indecent assault | 17 | 12 | 15 | 21 | 18 |
| Fraud | 156 | 90 | 101 | 160 | 115 |

3. If the incidents of fraud are omitted, which 2 divisions have the same number of reported criminal incidents?

A and B     C and D     B and C     D and E     B and E

Answer =

4. If the criminal statistics for the second quarter of the year show a 6 per cent increase, what would be the total number of criminal incidents in Division B for the half-year?

700          707          718          721          730

Answer =

The classes in a local primary school managed to raise the following amounts during a school year:

| Event | A | B | Class C | D | E |
|---|---|---|---|---|---|
| Raffle | £32 | £14 | £24 | £30 | £20 |
| Jumble sale | £20 | £24 | £24 | £34 | £32 |
| Car boot sale | £10 | £30 | £32 | £34 | £16 |
| Concert | £30 | £44 | £40 | £14 | £18 |
| Sponsored walk | £62 | £8 | £18 | £42 | £22 |
| Sports day | £8 | £24 | £24 | £28 | £14 |

5.   Which two classes raised the same amount as each other?

A and B      C and E      B and D      A and C      B and E

Answer =

6.   If each pupil in Class C raised £9 overall, with the exception of Tracey, who raised £18, how many pupils are there in Class C?

15                16                17                18                19

Answer =

7.   If Class A had raised only half the amount that they did for each event, and Class B had not taken part in the concert, which event would have raised the most money when funds from all classes are combined?

Raffle      Jumble      Car boot      Concert      Sponsored
              sale         sale                          walk

Answer =

Trends in the relative value on the market of selected groups of commodities (1990–94) are given below:

| Commodity | 1990 | 1991 | Year 1992 | 1993 | 1994 |
|---|---|---|---|---|---|
| Beverages | 95 | 92 | 86 | 72 | 76 |
| Cereals | 75 | 68 | 62 | 66 | 60 |
| Fats and oils | 76 | 70 | 68 | 62 | 58 |
| Timber | 82 | 76 | 100 | 98 | 96 |
| Metals | 80 | 62 | 64 | 84 | 88 |
| Minerals | 79 | 74 | 72 | 66 | 73 |

8. What is the average difference in the relative value of the 6 commodities in 1994 compared to 1990?

    +8            +4            – 5            – 6            +36

                                                Answer =

9. Which value showed the greatest amount of change in 1994 compared to 1990?

    Beverages   Cereals    Fats and oils    Timber    Metals

                                                Answer =

10. Which commodity showed the least variation in value over the period 1990–94?

    Beverages   Cereals    Fats and oils    Timber    Minerals

                                                Answer =

Monthly repayments (in £) on building society loans for different periods are shown in the following table.

| Loan | Years | | | |
| | 10 | 15 | 20 | 25 |
|---|---|---|---|---|
| 1,000 | 12.50 | 10.50 | 9.00 | 8.50 |
| 2,000 | 25.00 | 20.50 | 18.00 | 16.00 |
| 10,000 | 129.50 | 103.00 | 90.00 | 84.50 |
| 15,000 | 194.00 | 154.50 | 135.00 | 126.50 |
| 20,000 | 259.00 | 206.00 | 180.00 | 168.00 |

11. How much more would be paid on a loan of £20,000 taken out over 20 years compared to the same loan taken out over a period of 15 years?

£3,000        £4,250        £5,250        £6,120        £7,200

Answer =

12. What is the total amount repaid over 25 years of a loan of £15,000?

£22,300      £37,950      £45,300      £55,800      £66,100

Answer =

13. The monthly repayment on a loan of £15,000 over 20 years is reduced to £125.00. By how much would this reduce the total amount repaid on the loan over the full period?

£1,200        £2,400        £3,100        £3,900        £4,800

Answer =

The percentage increase in the annual retail prices of selected items in one store during the period 1982–87 is shown in the following table:

| Item | Price in 1982 | % Increase on 1982 price | | | | |
|------|------|------|------|------|------|------|
| | | 1983 | 1984 | 1985 | 1986 | 1987 |
| Washing machine | £340 | 2.4 | 4.6 | 5.8 | 7.6 | 8.8 |
| Dryer | £200 | 2.0 | 5.4 | 7.1 | 8.8 | 10.6 |
| Dishwasher | £240 | 2.8 | 4.6 | 6.4 | 7.9 | 9.8 |
| Vacuum cleaner | £125 | 2.7 | 4.8 | 6.3 | 7.7 | 9.3 |
| Stereo unit | £120 | 1.5 | 3.5 | 5.2 | 7.5 | 9.8 |
| TV | £265 | 2.0 | 4.5 | 6.2 | 7.9 | 9.5 |

14. How much more would a washing machine and dryer cost in 1987 compared to 1982?

£21.12          £31.12          £41.12          £51.12          £61.12

Answer =

15. In which 2 years was the combined annual percentage increase in the price of the 6 items the same?

1983 and     1985 and     1984 and     1985 and     1986 and
1984         1986         1986         1987         1987

Answer =

# Test 3

The 1990 A-level results showed that the percentage of candidates gaining pass grades A to E in selected subjects was as follows:

| Subject | Grade | | | | |
|---|---|---|---|---|---|
|  | A | B | C | D | E |
| Biology | 11.9 | 15.0 | 15.5 | 17.1 | 15.7 |
| Chemistry | 16.1 | 17.6 | 15.0 | 15.0 | 13.6 |
| Computing | 8.0 | 12.5 | 17.0 | 19.0 | 19.5 |
| English | 9.9 | 17.9 | 20.9 | 20.8 | 15.7 |
| Geography | 10.5 | 14.2 | 17.9 | 19.8 | 16.2 |
| Mathematics | 17.2 | 14.5 | 14.1 | 14.3 | 13.4 |

1.  What percentage of candidates failed to achieve a pass grade in Chemistry?

    207          21.7          22.7          23.7          24.7

                                              Answer =

2.  In which subject did the greatest percentage of candidates gain a pass grade?

    Biology   Chemistry   Computing   English   Geography

                                              Answer =

3.  If 46,540 candidates sat Biology and 42,440 candidates sat Geography, what was the approximate difference in the number of candidates who obtained a grade A in both subjects?

    800          900          1,000          1,100          1,200

                                              Answer =

The world prices of the main agricultural commodities (US$ per tonne) for the period 1985–89 were:

| Commodity | Year | | | | |
|---|---|---|---|---|---|
| | 1985 | 1986 | 1987 | 1988 | 1989 |
| Beef | 205 | 150 | 155 | 160 | 165 |
| Wheat | 178 | 136 | 112 | 135 | 140 |
| Butter | 124 | 84 | 75 | 90 | 98 |
| Maize | 120 | 75 | 68 | 80 | 82 |
| Sugar | 10 | 15 | 27 | 42 | 45 |
| Milk powder | 70 | 65 | 88 | 120 | 138 |

4.  In which 2 years would the total cost of buying 1 tonne of each of the 6 commodities have been the same?

| 1985 and 1989 | 1986 and 1987 | 1987 and 1988 | 1987 and 1989 | 1988 and 1989 |
|---|---|---|---|---|

Answer =

5.  Which 2 commodities showed the same change in price in 1989 compared to 1985?

| Beef and sugar | Maize and sugar | Beef and wheat | Wheat and maize | Wheat and sugar |
|---|---|---|---|---|

Answer =

6.  If prices had risen by 5 per cent per tonne during 1989 for all commodities except beef, which decreased by 12 per cent per tonne, what would the approximate difference in the overall cost of buying 1 tonne of each of the 6 commodities in 1990 have been compared to 1989?

| – 8 | – 5 | +2 | +5 | +8 |
|---|---|---|---|---|

Answer =

The Safe Travel Insurance Company issued the following table of premiums for holiday insurance in 1986:

|  | Premiums per person | | |
|---|---|---|---|
| Period of travel | Area A (UK) | Area B (Europe) | Area C (Worldwide) |
| 1–4 days | £3.50 | £5.50 | £16.00 |
| 5–8 days | £4.50 | £7.00 | £16.00 |
| 9–17 days | £5.50 | £10.00 | £21.50 |
| 18–23 days | £6.50 | £12.00 | £30.00 |
| 24–31 days | £7.50 | £15.50 | £34.50 |
| 32–62 days | £8.50 | £24.00 | £46.00 |

*Winter sports:* cover at 3 times these premiums
*Discount for children:* 20% reduction for each child under 14

7.  What would be the total premium paid by 2 adults and 2 children (both over 14) holidaying in the UK from 7 August to 17 August?

£18            £19            £20            £21            £22

Answer =

8.  What would be the total premium paid by 3 adults having a winter sports holiday in Europe from 7 to 14 January?

£33            £43            £53            £63            £73

Answer =

9.  If the insurance premiums are increased by 15 per cent what would be the new combined premium for a party of 4 adults taking a 21-day world holiday?

£128           £138           £148           £158           £168

Answer =

The percentage increase in prices since 1983 is shown in the following table:

**Average family
weekly expenditure**

| | (1983) | 1984 | 1985 | 1986 | 1987 | 1988 |
|---|---|---|---|---|---|---|
| | | (% Increase on 1983 rate) | | | | |
| Food | £40 | 2.3 | 4.8 | 7.8 | 11.6 | 15.6 |
| Alcohol | £9 | 0.3 | 2.3 | 7.9 | 17.1 | 21.7 |
| Housing | £16 | 3.3 | 8.4 | 14.0 | 20.5 | 28.5 |
| Fuel/light | £8 | 1.3 | 6.0 | 9.9 | 14.5 | 20.9 |
| Transport | £15 | 0.5 | 0.5 | 2.1 | 6.7 | 9.9 |
| Clothing | £12 | 2.0 | 3.5 | 4.9 | 7.0 | 9.9 |
| Other | £24 | 0.2 | 1.8 | 3.4 | 7.2 | 11.0 |
| Total | £124 | | | | | |

10. If an average family bought the same food in 1987 as they had in 1983, how much would their weekly food bill have cost in 1987?

   £44.64        £46.64        £48.64        £50.64        £52.64

   Answer =

11. If the Blue family buy 15 per cent more clothing and 5 per cent less food than the average family, by approximately how much will their weekly bill differ from that of the average family in 1983?

   +£1.80        +£0.30        – £0.20        – £0.80        – £1.80

   Answer =

12. If the average income has increased by 25 per cent in 1988, approximately how much will the average family have after paying for housing, fuel and light?

   £90.00      £108.72      £124.77      £138.10      £149.97

   Answer =

The local scout troops have managed to raise the following amounts in the 1990 fund raising season:

| | | | Troop | | |
|---|---|---|---|---|---|
| Event | Red | Blue | Green | Yellow | Brown |
| Jumble sale | £20 | £12 | £17 | £20 | £15 |
| Raffle | £15 | £17 | £17 | £22 | £21 |
| Car cleaning | £15 | £17 | £21 | £22 | £13 |
| Bob-a-job | £20 | £27 | £25 | £12 | £14 |
| Summer fête | £36 | £9 | £14 | £26 | £16 |
| Sponsored hike | £5 | £17 | £17 | £19 | £12 |

13. Which 2 troops raised the same amount as each other?

| Red and Blue | Yellow and Green | Brown and Red | Brown and Blue | Red and Green |
|---|---|---|---|---|

   Answer =

14. If each scout in Green Troop raised £14 overall, with the exception of Leroy, who raised £27, how many scouts are there in Green Troop?

   6            7            8            9            10

   Answer =

15. If Red Troop had raised only half the amount that they did for each event, and Blue Troop had not taken part in the Bob-a-job, which event would have raised the most money?

| Raffle | Bob-a-job | Car cleaning | Jumble sale | Summer fête |
|--------|-----------|--------------|-------------|-------------|

Answer =

## Test 4

A guide to personal loan repayment is given in the following table:

| Amount of loan | Monthly repayments for loans taken out over periods of 1 to 5 years | | | | |
|---|---|---|---|---|---|
| | 1 | 2 | 3 | 4 | 5 |
| £50 | £4.50 | £2.50 | £2.00 | £1.50 | £1.25 |
| £100 | £9.50 | £5.25 | £4.00 | £3.00 | £2.50 |
| £500 | £47.00 | £26.00 | £19.50 | £16.00 | £14.00 |
| £1,000 | £94.00 | £52.25 | £38.50 | £32.00 | £28.00 |
| £5,000 | £470.00 | £261.00 | £193.00 | £160.00 | £140.00 |
| £7,000 | £680.00 | £366.00 | £270.00 | £223.50 | £196.50 |

1. How much interest would be paid on a loan of £550 taken out over 3 years?

| £194 | £204 | £214 | £224 | £234 |
|------|------|------|------|------|

Answer =

2.  Mr Green takes out a loan of £5,000 over a 4-year period.
    How much would remain to be paid after 3 years' repay-
    ments have been made?

    £1,420          £1,920          £2,420          £2,920          £3,420

                                                    Answer =

3.  Mrs Brown took out and repaid a loan of £1,000 over a 5-
    year period. Approximately how much would she have
    saved if she had taken out and repaid the same loan over a
    3-year period?

    £100            £200            £300            £400            £500

                                                    Answer =

The basic 1989 holiday prices in £s per person were:

|         | Number of nights | | | | | |
|         | Period 1 | | Period 2 | | Period 3 | |
| Hotel   | 7 | 14 | 7 | 14 | 7 | 14 |
|---------|-----|-----|-----|-----|-----|-----|
| A       | 231 | 374 | 235 | 380 | 200 | 320 |
| B       | 174 | 260 | 178 | 291 | 140 | 210 |
| C       | 156 | 226 | 162 | 223 | 120 | 181 |
| D       | 150 | 218 | 156 | 222 | 145 | 178 |
| E       | 148 | 210 | 154 | 218 | 145 | 175 |

4.  Mr and Mrs Blue reserved a 14-night holiday for them-
    selves at Hotel B Period 2 and a 7-night holiday at the
    same hotel for their son and his fiancée during the same
    period. What was the combined cost of the holiday?

    £712            £794            £874            £938            £1,164

                                                    Answer =

5.  What would be the difference in cost of 4 people taking a 14-night holiday during Period 3 in Hotel A compared to the same period in Hotel E?

    £480          £520          £540          £580          £600

                                                Answer =

6.  The holiday prices are increased by 8 per cent for Period 1, and 12 per cent for Period 2. Approximately how much more would a holiday for 3 people staying at Hotel D for 14 nights in Period 2 cost, compared to 2 people staying in the same hotel for 14 nights in the same period, following the price rises?

    £200          £225          £250          £275          £300

                                                Answer =

The prices (per kilo) of selected food items in 5 supermarkets were:

|              |     | Supermarket |     |     |     |
|--------------|-----|-----|-----|-----|-----|
| Food item    | A   | B   | C   | D   | E   |
|              | £   | £   | £   | £   | £   |
| Stewing beef | 3.32 | 4.16 | 3.44 | 2.10 | 3.48 |
| Cheese       | 2.58 | 3.50 | 3.92 | 3.60 | 3.22 |
| Butter       | 2.24 | 2.08 | 2.80 | 2.52 | 3.24 |
| Tomatoes     | 0.90 | 1.52 | 1.08 | 0.92 | 0.72 |
| Bananas      | 1.38 | 0.86 | 0.80 | 0.76 | 1.00 |
| Apples       | 1.16 | 1.12 | 0.92 | 1.24 | 1.60 |

7.  In which supermarket would the cost of buying 1 kilo of each of the items be the least?

    A          B          C          D          E

                                                Answer =

8. Which food item shows the greatest range in price (ie difference between cheapest and most expensive) per kilo between the supermarkets?

Stewing beef   Cheese   Butter   Tomatoes   Bananas

Answer =

9. If supermarket A increases the price per kilo of stewing beef by 5 per cent and reduces the price per kilo of butter by 10 per cent, what would be the difference in cost of 2 kilos of stewing beef and 2 kilos of butter bought in supermarket A and the same items bought in supermarket C?

£0.89          £0.99          £1.09          £1.29          £1.49

Answer =

The increase in the number of new cars sold by 6 main dealers in 1985–90 was:

| Dealer | Sales in 1985 | Increase on 1985 sales | | | | |
|---|---|---|---|---|---|---|
| | | 1986 | 1987 | 1988 | 1989 | 1990 |
| A | 846 | 10 | 17 | 26 | 60 | 66 |
| B | 928 | 13 | 19 | 26 | 41 | 53 |
| C | 690 | 13 | 16 | 19 | 24 | 37 |
| D | 760 | 11 | 18 | 25 | 32 | 39 |
| E | 866 | 10 | 15 | 31 | 37 | 46 |
| F | 584 | 12 | 21 | 33 | 40 | 57 |
| Total sales | 4,674 | | | | | |

10. What was the combined total number of cars sold by dealers A and D in 1990?

1,671          1,681          1,691          1,701          1,711

Answer =

11. What was the average number of car sales per dealer in 1988 (to the nearest 25)?

725          750          775          800          825

Answer =

12. If, in comparison with 1985, the number of cars sold by dealer E in 1991 had increased by 8 per cent and the number of cars sold by the other dealers had increased by 10 per cent, what would the approximate increase have been in the combined number of cars sold by the dealers?

440          450          460          470          480

Answer =

The number of accidents attended by 6 emergency ambulance stations during a 5-month period was:

| Station | May | June | July | Aug | Sept |
| --- | --- | --- | --- | --- | --- |
| A | 21 | 20 | 22 | 36 | 37 |
| B | 32 | 33 | 30 | 52 | 38 |
| C | 36 | 36 | 38 | 48 | 33 |
| D | 31 | 32 | 34 | 37 | 36 |
| E | 26 | 26 | 25 | 29 | 22 |
| F | 34 | 38 | 36 | 47 | 36 |

13. What was the percentage increase (rounded to the nearest whole number) in the number of emergencies attended during September compared to May?

8%          10%          12%          14%          16%

Answer =

14. What was the approximate average increase in the number of emergencies attended by all 6 stations in August compared to July?

    9              11              13              15              17

                                                    Answer =

15. If, based on the September figures, the statistics for the month of October show that the number of emergencies attended by Stations D and F have increased by 25 per cent, and the number attended by Station B decreased by 16 per cent, what would be the difference in the total number of emergencies attended by these three stations in October compared to September?

    – 6            +6            +12            +18            +24

                                                    Answer =

# Data interpretation tests: answers

## Test 1

1. 290
2. B
3. B
4. April
5. A and C
6. B and E
7. A and D
8. 7
9. B
10. C and E
11. D
12. C
13. A and F
14. +0.1
15. +3

## Test 2

1. B
2. 12
3. D and E
4. 721
5. A and C
6. 17
7. Jumble sale
8. − 6
9. Beverages
10. Minerals
11. £6,120
12. £37,950
13. £2,400
14. £51.12
15. 1986 and 1987

## Test 3

1. 22.7
2. English
3. 1,100
4. 1986 and 1987
5. Wheat and maize
6. +5
7. £22
8. £63
9. £138
10. £44.64
11. −£0.20
12. £124.77
13. Red and Green
14. 7
15. Raffle

## Test 4

1. £224
2. £1,920
3. £300
4. £938
5. £580
6. £250
7. D
8. Stewing beef
9. £1.49
10. 1,711
11. 800
12. 450
13. 12%
14. 11
15. +12

# Data Interpretation Tests (2)

The data interpretation tests provided here are similar to those given in Chapter 5 in that they are multiple-choice tests of a type commonly used in personnel selection. However, in this chapter, the numerical data upon which the questions are based are given a variety of forms, ie different types of graphs and diagrams as well as statistical tables. Three practice tests are provided below, each consisting of 25 questions. You should allow yourself 25 minutes to complete each test. As before, your aim should be to work as quickly and as accurately as possible. Try to answer as many of the questions as you can in the time available.

Each test consists of five sets of numerical data presented in the form of graphs or tables, each of which is followed by five questions. For each question there are five possible answers. Your task is to work out which is the correct answer to each question using the relevant data. You should record your answer in the space provided.

**Example**
Five shops averaged the following monthly sales of items of furniture in one calendar year.

| Items | Shops | | | | |
|---|---|---|---|---|---|
| | **A** | **B** | **C** | **D** | **E** |
| Dining tables | 18 | 20 | 24 | 17 | 21 |
| Dining chairs | 72 | 86 | 96 | 72 | 92 |
| Bookcases | 19 | 23 | 21 | 20 | 14 |
| Sofas | 32 | 41 | 45 | 28 | 39 |
| Beds | 23 | 28 | 26 | 27 | 15 |

1.  Which 2 shops sold the same total number of items?

    A and B      C and D      B and C      D and E      A and D

    Answer = A and D

# Test 1

Figure 6.1  The number (in hundreds) of pupils at 5 rural schools from 1991–95

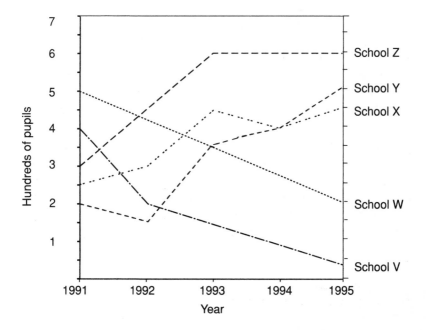

1.  Which school had the most pupils in 1991?

    V           W           X           Y           Z

                                        Answer =

2.  What was the total number (in hundreds) of pupils at these
    5 schools in 1993?

    14          16          19          20          1,900

                                        Answer =

3.  Which school showed a decrease in its pupil population at
    a constant rate from 1991 to 1995?

    V           W           X           Y           Z

                                        Answer =

4.  Which school had the same number of pupils in three
    consecutive years?

    V           W           X           Y           Z

                                        Answer =

5.  Which school increased its pupil population in each of the
    years between 1992 and 1995?

    V           W           X           Y           Z

                                        Answer =

The number of televisions (TVs), video recorders (VRs) and radio (Rs) sold by 5 shops in April and September, 1995:

| Shop | April | | | September | | |
|------|------|-----|----|------|-----|----|
|      | TVs  | VRs | Rs | TVs  | VRs | Rs |
| V    | 20   | 14  | 0  | 90   | 120 | 96 |
| W    | 16   | 12  | 2  | 70   | 104 | 68 |
| X    | 12   | 14  | 0  | 64   | 110 | 66 |
| Y    | 20   | 16  | 0  | 104  | 150 | 86 |
| Z    | 16   | 24  | 0  | 92   | 160 | 92 |

6.  In September 1995, which shop sold the same number of televisions as it sold radios?

V          W          X          Y          Z

Answer =

7.  In April 1995, one shop had the least difference in its sales of televisions and video recorders. Which shop was it?

V          W          X          Y          Z

Answer =

8.  The number of video recorders sold by one shop in September 1995 was 6 times its sales of televisions in April 1995. Which shop ws it?

V          W          X          Y          Z

Answer =

9. Which shop had the greatest increase in the actual number of video recorders sold in September 1995 as compared with April 1995?

V          W          X          Y          Z

Answer =

10. What was the percentage increase in the total sales of televisions in September 1995 as compared with April 1995?

42%        400%        500%        600%        5,000%

Answer =

The number of pupils who passed and failed GCE A-Level English examinations in 5 schools from 1994 to 1998:

| School | Examination Results | 1994 | 1995 | 1996 | 1997 | 1998 |
|--------|--------------------|------|------|------|------|------|
| 1 | Passed | 25 | 19 | 21 | 16 | 28 |
|   | Failed | 8 | 7 | 9 | 5 | 10 |
| 2 | Passed | 7 | 6 | 7 | 15 | 13 |
|   | Failed | 4 | 4 | 5 | 9 | 7 |
| 3 | Passed | 4 | 4 | 4 | 6 | 3 |
|   | Failed | 2 | 3 | 5 | 4 | 2 |
| 4 | Passed | 12 | 12 | 11 | 25 | 15 |
|   | Failed | 6 | 5 | 6 | 11 | 8 |
| 5 | Passed | 8 | 9 | 13 | 17 | 16 |
|   | Failed | 5 | 4 | 6 | 6 | 7 |

11. What was the total number of pupils who attempted the GCE A-Level English examination in 1994 and 1995?

197          154          200          128          225

Answer =

12. In which year did more pupils fail than pass the GCE A-Level English examination at School 3?

    1994          1995          1996          1997          1998

                                              Answer =

13. Which school had its least number of passes in GCE A-Level English in 1996 followed by its greatest number of passes in 1997?

    1             2             3             4             5

                                              Answer =

14. Of the total number of pupils who passed the GCE A-Level English examination in 1998, what percentage was from School 4?

    7             10            15            17            20

                                              Answer =

15. What was the ratio of the number of pupils who failed the GCE A-Level English examination in School 3 in 1995 to the number who passed it in School 2 in 1997?

    1:6           1:5           1:4           4:15          1:3

                                              Answer =

Figure 6.2 The number (in hundreds) of female and male shoppers on 1 June 1998 at 5 supermarkets (V, W, X, Y and Z).

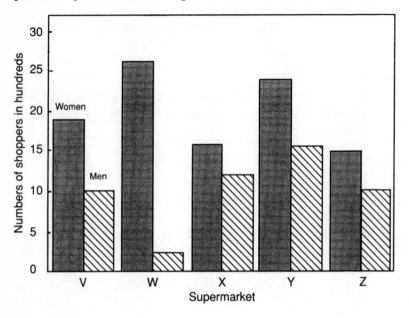

16. Which supermarket had the greatest number of shoppers on 1 June 1998?

    V          W          X          Y          Z

                                              Answer =

17. Which 2 of these 5 supermarkets had the same number of male shoppers on 1 June 1998?

    V          W          X          Y          Z

                                              Answer =

18. What was the total number (in thousands) of female shoppers in these 5 supermarkets on 1 June 1998?

    10              15          50          100         10,000

                                                Answer =

19. What proportion of the total number of male shoppers in these 5 supermarkets on 1 June 1998 was at Supermarket Z?

    1/20            1/15        8/75        1/5         8/25

                                                Answer =

20. On 5 June 1998 the number of women and men shoppers in Supermarket Y increased by 25 per cent and 150 per cent respectively over the number of shoppers on 1 June 1998. What was the total number of shoppers (in hundreds) in Supermarket Y on 5 June 1998?

    30              40          46          62          70

                                                Answer =

Figure 6.3  The number of computers sold by 5 salespeople (A, B, C, D and E) in each month of 1998

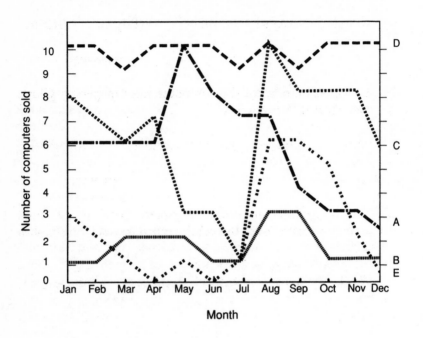

21. Whose computer sales were the most consistent throughout the year?

    A          B          C          D          E

                                        Answer =

22. Which salesperson sold the same number of computers in each of 4 consecutive months?

    A          B          C          D          E

                                        Answer =

23. In which month did 3 of the salespeople sell the same number of computers?

   March        April        May        July        August

                                             Answer =

24. In which month did the computer sales of person C and person A differ most?

   May       June       July       October       November

                                             Answer =

25. Which month showed the largest increase in total computer sales over the total computer sales one month before?

   April       May       July       August       November

                                             Answer =

## Test 2

The number of residents at 5 hotels (V, W, X, Y and Z) on 1 February and 1 July 1998:

**1 February 1998**

| Hotel | Female adults | Male adults | Female children | Male children |
|-------|--------------|-------------|-----------------|---------------|
| V | 32 | 64 | 8 | 11 |
| W | 11 | 28 | 3 | 2 |
| X | 47 | 84 | 14 | 7 |
| Y | 22 | 42 | 5 | 6 |
| Z | 63 | 104 | 18 | 23 |

## 1 July 1998

| Hotel | Female adults | Male adults | Female children | Male children |
|-------|--------------|-------------|-----------------|---------------|
| V | 41 | 73 | 16 | 14 |
| W | 18 | 37 | 7 | 6 |
| X | 47 | 92 | 12 | 17 |
| Y | 37 | 59 | 19 | 13 |
| Z | 81 | 112 | 26 | 20 |

1.  Which of the 5 hotels had the same number of female adult residents on 1 February 1998 as it did on 1 July 1998?

    V          W          X          Y          Z

                                        Answer =

2.  In which hotel was the total number of adult residents on 1 July 1998 three times greater than the total number of children in residence?

    V          W          X          Y          Z

                                        Answer =

3.  The number of male adult residents at one hotel on 1 February 1998 was 7 times its number of female children residents on 1 July. Which hotel was it?

    V          W          X          Y          Z

                                        Answer =

4. Which hotel had the greatest increase in the total number of adult residents on 1 July 1998 compared with 1 February of that year?

V              W              X              Y              Z

Answer =

5. What was the percentage increase in the total number of female adult residents in all 5 hotels on 1 July 1998 compared with 1 February 1998?

28              17              49              25              31

Answer=

Cinema admissions and takings in Great Britain 1969–79:

**Number of admissions (millions)**

| 1969 | 1970 | 1971 | 1972 | 1973 | 1974 | 1975 | 1976 | 1977 | 1978 | 1979 |
|------|------|------|------|------|------|------|------|------|------|------|
| 215 | 193 | 176 | 157 | 134 | 138 | 116 | 104 | 103 | 126 | 112 |

**Average price of admission (pence)**

| 1969 | 1970 | 1971 | 1972 | 1973 | 1974 | 1975 | 1976 | 1977 | 1978 | 1979 |
|------|------|------|------|------|------|------|------|------|------|------|
| 26.8 | 30.6 | 34.2 | 37.9 | 43.2 | 50.1 | 61.2 | 73.0 | 82.6 | 93.7 | 113.4 |

Regional analysis of admissions (for selected regions):

| | Admissions (thousands) | | Average price of admission (pence) | |
|---|---|---|---|---|
| | 1978 | 1979 | 1978 | 1979 |
| Great Britain | 126,146 | 111,859 | 93.7 | 113.40 |
| North Yorkshire & Humberside | 6,531 | 5,774 | 92.7 | 97.9 |
| Yorkshire & Humberside | 9,115 | 7,972 | 89.0 | 108.5 |
| East Midlands | 5,929 | 5,290 | 85.8 | 102.5 |
| East Anglia | 4,001 | 3,502 | 88.0 | 106.3 |
| South East: Greater London Council area | 26,629 | 23,815 | 124.1 | 151.8 |
| Outer Metropolitan area | 13,200 | 11,763 | 85.3 | 103.7 |
| West Midlands | 8,083 | 7,765 | 83.8 | 100.9 |

6.  In which year did the maximum increase in the average price of cinema admissions in Great Britain occur when compared with the previous year?

    1973          1975          1977          1978          1979

    Answer =

7.  In 1970, the average price of cinema admissions in Great Britain was 30.6 pence. By which year had the average price increased by exactly 100 per cent?

    1972          1973          1974          1975          1976

    Answer =

8.  What was the average annual decrease in cinema admissions (in millions) in Great Britain between 1969 and 1979?

    9.36        103,000        1.03        10.30        103

    Answer =

9.  What percentage (approximately) of the total cinema admissions in Great Britain in 1978 was in the Greater London Council area of the South East?

    27%        12%        21%        25%        31%

    Answer =

10. What would the average price in pence of cinema admissions in Great Britain in 1979 have been if the Greater London Council and the Outer Metropolitan areas of the South East region had been excluded from the calculation?

    115.2        103.2        105.2        06.3        104.5

    Answer =

Figure 6.4   The average monthly temperatures (in degrees centigrade) for five weather stations in the northern hemisphere

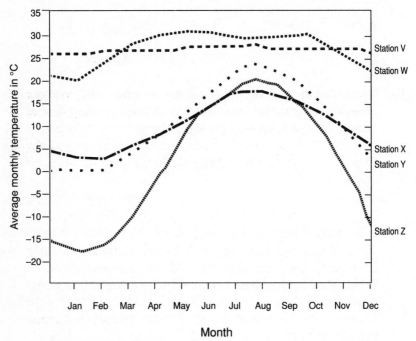

11. Which of the 5 weather stations has the smallest annual range of temperature (ie the difference between the average temperature of its coldest month and its warmest month)?

V          W          X          Y          Z

Answer =

12. In which of the 5 weather stations is the average monthly temperature 2 degrees centigrade higher in December than it is in January?

    V          W          X          Y          Z

                                        Answer =

13. Assume that plants begin to grow when the average monthly temperature rises above 6 degrees centigrade and ceases when the average monthly temperature falls below that figure. This period of plant growth is known as the 'growing season'. Which of the 5 stations has the shortest growing season?

    V          W          X          Y          Z

                                        Answer =

14. What is the ratio of months with average monthly temperatures of 5 degrees centigrade and below to those with average monthly temperatures above 5 degrees centigrade at Station Y?

    1:4          3:12          1:2          5:7          3:9

                                        Answer =

15. What is the average monthly temperature in degrees centigrade for January for all 5 weather stations combined?

    13.6          6.4          4.8          –6.4          10.0

                                        Answer =

Figure 6.5    Number of houses built by different sectors in the United Kingdom, 1971–75.

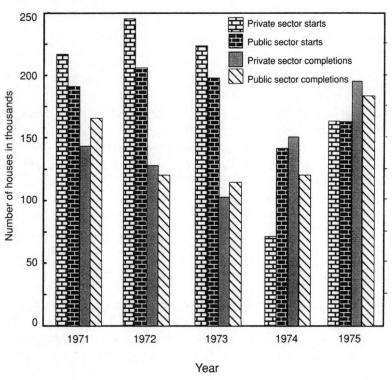

16. In which of the 5 years in the period 1971–75 did the greatest number of private sector housing starts occur?

1971            1972            1973            1974            1975

Answer =

17. In which 2 of the 5 years during the period 1971–75 were the same number of public sector houses completed?

    1971            1972            1973            1974            1975

                                                    Answer =

18. What was the total number (in thousands) of private sector housing completions in the 5 year period 1971–75?

    9,100        9,100,000        900            710            910

                                                    Answer =

19. What was the percentage (to the nearest per cent) increase in private sector housing starts from 1971 to 1972?

    9%            11%            22%            19%            100%

                                                    Answer =

20. What proportion of the total number of housing starts in 1974 was in the public sector?

    1/2            1/3            10/15            3/5            2/3

                                                    Answer =

Figure 6.6　Number of employees in 5 companies in the United Kingdom (in thousands) and in the North (in hundreds)

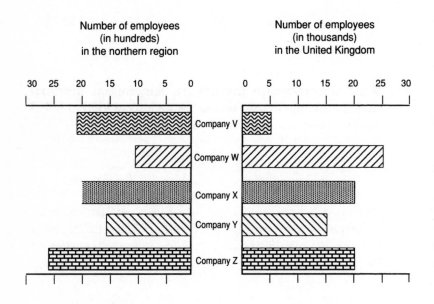

21. What is the total number of employees (in thousands) in the United Kingdom of Company Z?

　　22.5　　　　2,250　　　　20,250　　　　20　　　　20,000

　　　　　　　　　　　　　　　　　　　　　　Answer =

22. How many (in thousands) of the United Kingdom employees of Company X work in regions outside the North?

　　1,800　　　　20　　　　18　　　　18,000　　　　2,000

　　　　　　　　　　　　　　　　　　　　　　Answer =

23. Which of the 5 companies has the greatest proportion of its employees working in the North?

V              W              X              Y              Z

Answer =

24. What percentage (to the nearest per cent) of the total number of employees in the United Kingdom of all 5 companies is employed by Company W?

18%          23%          15%          28%          31%

Answer          =

25. If the total number of employees in the United Kingdom of Company X was to increase by 20 per cent and Company Y by 80 per cent, what would be the total combined workforce (in thousands) of the 2 companies?

46              51              54              59              62

Answer =

## Test 3

Number of new female and male employees engaged by 5 employers from 1994 to 1998:

| Employer | Gender of New Employees | 1994 | 1995 | 1996 | 1997 | 1998 |
|---|---|---|---|---|---|---|
| V | Female | 4 | 4 | 5 | 11 | 12 |
|   | Male | 7 | 6 | 7 | 15 | 15 |
| W | Female | 10 | 11 | 9 | 17 | 15 |
|   | Male | 12 | 12 | 11 | 25 | 14 |
| X | Female | 87 | 68 | 71 | 58 | 93 |
|   | Male | 88 | 79 | 87 | 85 | 88 |
| Y | Female | 5 | 7 | 6 | 11 | 10 |
|   | Male | 6 | 4 | 8 | 14 | 20 |
| Z | Female | 2 | 2 | 3 | 3 | 3 |
|   | Male | 4 | 4 | 2 | 6 | 3 |

1.  What was the total number of new employees (female and male) in all 5 companies in 1994 and 1995?

    322          348          392          422          448

                                         Answer =

2.  Which of the 5 companies took on a bigger total of new employees in 1995 than in 1994?

    V          W          X          Y          Z

                                         Answer =

3.  What was the average number of new female employees per company in 1997?

    11          17          20          22          25

                                         Answer =

4.  Of the total number of new male employees in all 5 companies in 1998, what percentage was employed collectively by companies V, W and Y?

    31%          35%          39%          41%          45%

    Answer =

5.  What was the ratio of new female employees in Company Y in 1994 to the number of new male employees in Company X in 1997?

    1:15          3:29          1:17          6:85          1:19

    Answer =

Figure 6.7   Building society net receipts and mortgage advances (in £ millions), August–December 1988

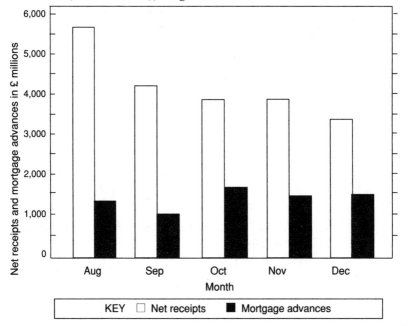

6.  In which 2 of the 5 months were the same amount of building society mortgage advances made?

    August    September    October    November    December

                                    Answer =

7.  In which month was there the greatest excess of building society net receipts over mortgage advances?

    August    September    October    November    December

                                    Answer =

8.  What was the total amount (in millions of pounds) of building society mortgage advances over the 5-month period from August to December 1988?

    6,200      7,000      70,000,000      7,800      78,000

                                    Answer =

9.  What was the ratio of building society mortgage advances to net receipts in December 1988?

    1:8          1:6          1:4          1:3          2:3

                                    Answer =

10. Assume that, by the end of January 1989, the building society net receipts and mortgage advances had fallen by 50 per cent and 25 per cent, respectively, compared with the figures for December 1988. What would the building society turnover (the figure obtained by adding net receipts to mortgage advances) have been for January 1989 (in millions of pounds)?

    1,800      2,200      24,000,000      2,400      24,000

                                    Answer =

Figure 6.8   Average monthly rainfall in millimetres at 5 weather stations in the northern hemisphere

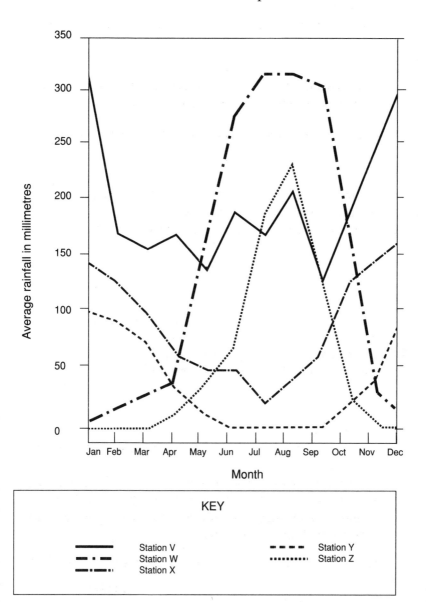

11.

In which month at Station V does the lowest average monthly
    rainfall total occur?

March        May          July          September    November

Answer =

12. In how many months at Station Z is the average monthly
    rainfall total 0 millimetres?

3            4            5            6            7

Answer =

13. In which of the 5 weather stations does the average
    monthly rainfall exceed 150 millimetres from May to
    October?

V            W            X            Y            Z

Answer =

14. In which of the 5 weather stations does the average
    monthly rainfall fall below 50 millimetres for 8 months of
    the year?

V            W            X            Y            Z

Answer =

15. In which of the 5 weather stations is there the greatest
    difference between the month with the lowest average
    monthly rainfall total and the month with the largest
    average rainfall total?

V            W            X            Y            Z

Answer =

Figure 6.9    Sales (in thousands) of 5 books during the period
1993–97

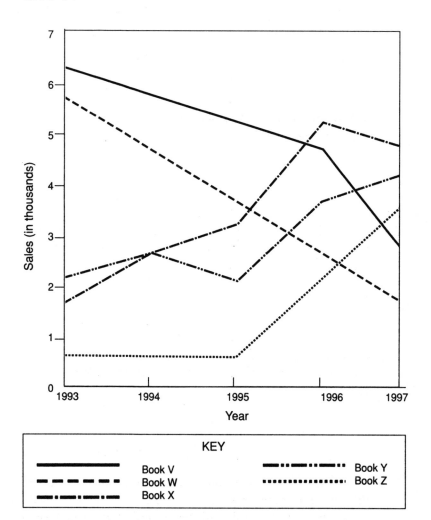

16. Which of the 5 books had uniform sales for 3 years before increasing for the next 2 years at a constant rate?

V          W          X          Y          Z

Answer =

17. Which of the 5 books had the least difference between its annual sales in 1993 compared with its sales in 1997?

V          W          X          Y          Z

Answer =

18. What was the difference (in thousands) between the total sales for all 5 books in 1994 compared with 1996?

1.5          2,000          2          2.5          2,500

Answer =

19. What percentage of the total annual sales for all 5 books in 1993 was contributed by the combined sales of Book V and Book Y?

33%          39%          45%          50%          55%

Answer =

20. What proportion of the total annual sales for the period 1993–97 of Book W occurred in 1995?

1/5          2/5          1/4          2/9          1/6

Answer =

Service industry grants by regions in 1974 and 1977

| Region | Year | Applications submitted | | Value (in thousands of pounds) | Number of jobs created |
|---|---|---|---|---|---|
| | | Number submitted | Number offered | | |
| V | 1974 | 14 | 6 | 66 | 134 |
| | 1977 | 12 | 3 | 14 | 15 |
| W | 1974 | 19 | 5 | 155 | 211 |
| | 1977 | 25 | 8 | 56 | 43 |
| X | 1974 | 7 | 1 | 28 | 21 |
| | 1977 | 32 | 13 | 828 | 455 |
| Y | 1974 | 26 | 11 | 221 | 495 |
| | 1977 | 29 | 17 | 2,012 | 1,302 |
| Z | 1974 | 5 | 0 | 0 | 0 |
| | 1977 | 38 | 14 | 315 | 801 |

21. Which of the 5 regions had the greatest difference between the number of grant applications that it submitted in 1974 compared with 1977?

V          W          X          Y          Z

Answer =

22. What was the difference between the total number of grant applications submitted by the 5 regions in 1974 compared with 1977?

58          65          69          76          80

Answer =

23. What was the average value (in thousands of pounds) per region of the service industry grants given to the 5 regions in 1977?

615          630          640,000          645          650

Answer =

24. Of the total number of jobs it was estimated that the service industry grants would create in the 5 regions in 1974, what proportion was it estimated would be in Region X?

1/34            1/40            1/41            1/43            1/47

Answer =

25. In which of the 5 regions in 1977 was the average cost per job created by means of service industry grants the highest?

V            W            X            Y            Z

Answer =

# Data interpretation tests: answers

## Test 1

| | | |
|---|---|---|
| 1. W | 10. 400% | 19. 1/5 |
| 2. 19 | 11. 154 | 20. 70 |
| 3. W | 12. 1996 | 21. D |
| 4. Z | 13. 4 | 22. A |
| 5. Y | 14. 20 | 23. July |
| 6. Z | 15. 1.5 | 24. May |
| 7. X | 16. Y | 25. August |
| 8. V | 17. V and Z | |
| 9. Z | 18. 10 | |

## Test 2

| | | |
|---|---|---|
| 1. X | 10. 103.2 | 18. 710 |
| 2. Y | 11. V | 19. 11% |
| 3. X | 12. Y | 20. 2/3 |
| 4. Y | 13. Z | 21. 20 |
| 5. 28% | 14. 1:2 | 22. 18 |
| 6. 1979 | 15. 6.4 | 23. V |
| 7. 1975 | 16. 1972 | 24. 28% |
| 8. 10.30 | 17. 1972 and | 25. 51 |
| 9. 21% |     1974 | |

## Test 3

| | | |
|---|---|---|
| 1. 422 | 9. 1:3 | 18. 2.5 |
| 2. W | 10. 220 | 19. 50% |
| 3. 20 | 11. September | 20. 1/5 |
| 4. 35% | 12. 5 | 21. Z |
| 5. 1:17 | 13. W | 22. 65 |
| 6. November and | 14. Y | 23. 645 |
|    December | 15. W | 24. 1/41 |
| 7. August | 16. Z | 25. X |
| 8. 4,800 | 17. Y | |

# Number Sequence Tests

The number sequence tests that follow are similar to ones that are commonly used in personnel selection tests. Working through these tests will help you to develop your numerical reasoning and understand the principles on which these tests are constructed. This will then help improve your performance when you are required to take such tests.

The first three tests contain 24 questions and you should attempt to do these in 12 minutes. Speed and accuracy are important in these, as in all tests, and in order to help develop these you should also attempt to complete the fourth test in 12 minutes, even though it contains 30 items. Before you begin to time yourself on one of the tests, you should study these instructions and the examples carefully.

Each line contains a sequence of numbers but one number is missing and has been replaced with an 'xx'. In all cases the answer is a two digit number. Your task in each case is to indicate what the missing number should be.

**Examples**

1.  3   7   11   xx   19          Answer = 15

2.  1   2   4   8   xx           Answer = 16

3.  6   1   7   12   3   15   2   10   xx      Answer = 12

When you have completed a test you should go back over it and make a note of the principles on which each item is constructed, as indicated below.

In Example 1, the numbers increase by +4:

$$3 (+4) = 7 (+4) = 11 (+4) = 15 (+4) = 19$$

The missing number (or xx), therefore, is 15.

In Example 2, the numbers increase by a factor of 2, as follows:

$$1 (\times 2) = 2 (\times 2) = 4 (\times 2) = 8 (\times 2) = 16$$

The missing number (or xx), therefore, is 16.

In Example 3, the numbers are in groups of three and in each group of three, the second number added to the first equals the third. So:

$$6 + 1 = 7 \quad 12 + 3 = 15 \quad 2 + 10 = 12$$

The missing number (or xx), therefore, is 12.

If, after you have completed a practice test, you work through it in this way, you will soon grasp the principles on which tests such as these are constructed. An understanding of the principles on which these tests are constructed will provide you with a mental checklist to work through when you take this sort of test. This should help to reduce any feelings of panic if you do not see the number sequence, or the way in which the numbers are related, straight away.

A number of worked examples are provided at the end of this chapter. We would suggest that you now proceed with the practice tests following the guidelines given below.

- ■ Attempt the first practice test in the time limit of 12 minutes.
- ■ Mark your answers and give yourself a score out of 24.
- ■ Go over the test and write in the principles on which each item is constructed.
- ■ Repeat steps given above with Test 2 and Test 3. This will help to consolidate your learning as you proceed.
- ■ If you feel that you are progressing satisfactorily proceed to attempt Test 4. Use the worked examples provided at the end of the chapter for reference and revision purposes before taking a real selection test.
- ■ If at this stage you are still experiencing difficulties go carefully through the worked examples to establish an understanding of the principle on which each of the items is constructed.
- ■ When you feel that you have a grasp of this proceed to tackle the fourth practice test.

# Number sequences

## Test 1

*Answer*

1.   3  10  xx  24  31                          xx =

2.   24  19  15  xx  10                        xx =

3. 2  4  12  xx  240                                    xx =

4. 7  15  23  26  26  23  xx  7                          xx =

5. 3  5  9  17  xx                                       xx =

6. 108  93  82  71  71  xx  93  108                      xx =

7. 5  11  23  47  xx                                     xx =

8. 8  17  35  xx  143                                    xx =

9. 9  27  28  xx  85  255                                xx =

10. 11  9  18  16  32  xx                                xx =

11. 217  14    184  14    417  34    385  xx             xx =

12. 18  24  28  36  36  28  xx                           xx =

13. 124  16    592  61    xx3  20    416  47             xx =

14. 628  54    311  30    627  55    298  xx             xx =

15. xx8  72    374  41    262  28    381  39             xx =

16. 216  54  xx  9                                       xx =

17. 840  168  xx  14                                     xx =

18. 22  12  10    35  xx  16    34  23  11               xx =

19. xx  27  26    42  14  28    54  11  43               xx =

20. 47  22  25    36  14  22    27  15  xx               xx =

21. 6230 83   1472 59   3152 xx   9061 97      xx =

22. 4216 67   2531 74   6151 76   6132   xx      xx =

23. 6 6 8   12   12 24 20 xx 36                     xx =

24. 17 9 16   12 14 15 xx 18 7                     xx =

## Test 2

*Answer*

1. 7 12 17 xx 27                                    xx =

2. 22 21 19 16 xx                                   xx =

3. 1 2 6 xx 120                                     xx =

4. 47 43 32 27 27 32 43 xx                          xx =

5. 6 13 27 xx 111                                   xx =

6. 8 11 16 25 29 29 xx 16                           xx =

7. 54 46 42 xx 39                                   xx =

8. 12 23 45 xx 177                                  xx =

9. 4 8 9 18 19 xx                                   xx =

10. 615 56   374 33   219 xx   417 34               xx =

11. 12 9   27 24   72 xx                            xx =

12. 382 36   571 56   489 xx 593 56                 xx =

13. 127 19   594 63   xx8 25   406 46          xx =

14. xx7 53   301 29   727 65   290 29          xx =

15. 1320 264 66 xx                             xx =

16. 23 11 12   35 xx 16   34 13 21             xx =

17. xx 27 16   52 24 28   34 11 23             xx =

18. 46 22 68   39 10 49   27 15 xx             xx =

19. 6234 87   1872 99   2122 xx   8061 87      xx =

20. 2216 47   2634 87   7172 89   6232 xx      xx =

21. 6 7 14   15 30 xx                          xx =

22. 8 24 23 xx 68 204                          xx =

23. 16 8 14 16 10 xx 2 192                     xx =

24. 26 84 29 72 35 60 47 xx                    xx =

## Test 3

*Answer*

1. 4 7 10 xx 16                               xx =

2. 16 24 xx 40 48                             xx =

3. 38 36 32 xx 8                              xx =

4. 60 44 36 32 xx                             xx =

5. 80  60  42  xx  12                          xx =

6. 16  20  28  44  xx                          xx =

7. 7  9  13  16  17  17  16  xx                xx =

8. 8  17  35  xx  143                          xx =

9. 4  9  19  39  xx                            xx =

10. 4  6  12  14  15  15  xx  12               xx =

11. 8  15  29  xx  113                         xx =

12. 10  19  37  xx  145                        xx =

13. 24  29  36  41  41  36  xx  24             xx =

14. 197  12    865  81    263  xx    412  39   xx =

15. 583  55    627  55    196  13  xx4  34     xx =

16. 193  22    318  39    327  xx    506  56   xx =

17. 199  28    156  21    xx5  48    462  48   xx =

18. 62  27  35    48  17  31    39  12  xx     xx =

19. 83  14  69    37  xx  15    56  19  37     xx =

20. 27  16  11    xx  11  18    49  21  28     xx =

21. 26  13  39    34  xx  57    19  17  36     xx =

22. 2563  79    8123  95    2624  xx    7025  77    xx =

23. 3  5  20  22  88  xx  360                                    xx =

24. 1851  96    1652  77    3152  xx    8140  94        xx =

## Test 4

*Answer*

1.  17  24  xx  38  45                                          xx =

2.  21  30  39  xx  57                                          xx =

3.  10  16  xx  28  34                                          xx =

4.  74  71  65  53  xx                                          xx =

5.  80  70  61  53  xx                                          xx =

6.  57  49  42  xx  31                                          xx =

7.  6  13  27  xx  111                                          xx =

8.  7  15  31  xx  127                                          xx =

9.  11  23  47  xx  191                                         xx =

10. 9  17  33  xx  129                                          xx =

11. 7  13  25  49  xx                                           xx =

12. 12  23  45  xx  177                                         xx =

13. 191  18    468  38    514  47    301  xx        xx =

14. 624  58    326  26    152  13    377  xx        xx =

15. 265 21   486 42   625 xx 427 35          xx =

16. 478 55   182 20   264 xx   305 35        xx =

17. 625 67   324 36   471 xx   247 31        xx =

18. 376 43   295 34   587 xx   365 41        xx =

19. 45 17 28   49 xx 20   28 11 17           xx =

20. 58 11 47   38 xx 23   82 43 39           xx =

21. 35 24 11   46 xx 22   66 27 39           xx =

22. 24 16 40   46 27 73   61 29 xx           xx =

23. 64 18 82   16 xx 35   37 49 86           xx =

24. 77 14 91   41 18 59   18 xx 37           xx =

25. 8036 89   3372 69   5231 xx   1132 25    xx =

26. 3471 78   4213 64   4126 58   2417 xx    xx =

27. 8132 95   2433 66   2216 xx   1426 58    xx =

28. 3478 4589 23xx 1256                      xx =

29. 3467 1245 45xx 2356                      xx =

30. 1618 1921 2224 25xx                      xx =

# Number sequence tests: answers

## Test 1

| | | |
|---|---|---|
| 1. 17 | 9. 84 | 17. 42 |
| 2. 12 | 10. 30 | 18. 19 |
| 3. 48 | 11. 33 | 19. 53 |
| 4. 15 | 12. 24 | 20. 12 |
| 5. 33 | 13. 17 | 21. 47 |
| 6. 82 | 14. 21 | 22. 75 |
| 7. 95 | 15. 64 | 23. 48 |
| 8. 71 | 16. 18 | 24. 11 |

## Test 2

| | | |
|---|---|---|
| 1. 22 | 9. 38 | 17. 43 |
| 2. 12 | 10. 12 | 18. 42 |
| 3. 24 | 11. 69 | 19. 34 |
| 4. 47 | 12. 39 | 20. 85 |
| 5. 55 | 13. 17 | 21. 31 |
| 6. 25 | 14. 60 | 22. 69 |
| 7. 40 | 15. 22 | 23. 48 |
| 8. 89 | 16. 19 | 24. 48 |

## Test 3

| | | |
|---|---|---|
| 1. 13 | 9. 79 | 17. 43 |
| 2. 32 | 10. 14 | 18. 27 |
| 3. 24 | 11. 57 | 19. 22 |
| 4. 30 | 12. 73 | 20. 29 |
| 5. 26 | 13. 29 | 21. 23 |
| 6. 76 | 14. 23 | 22. 86 |
| 7. 13 | 15. 38 | 23. 90 |
| 8. 71 | 16. 39 | 24. 47 |

## Test 4

| | | |
|---|---|---|
| 1. 31 | 11. 97 | 21. 24 |
| 2. 48 | 12. 89 | 22. 90 |
| 3. 22 | 13. 29 | 23. 19 |
| 4. 29 | 14. 30 | 24. 19 |
| 5. 46 | 15. 57 | 25. 74 |
| 6. 36 | 16. 30 | 26. 68 |
| 7. 55 | 17. 48 | 27. 47 |
| 8. 63 | 18. 65 | 28. 67 |
| 9. 95 | 19. 29 | 29. 78 |
| 10. 65 | 20. 15 | 30. 27 |

# Number sequences: worked examples

All problems in the number sequence tests are variations on the worked examples given below.

1.   3  10  xx  24  31          | Answer = 17 |

In this problem each number in the sequence is increased by a number that remains the same for each increase:

$$3 (+7) = 10 (+7) = 17 (+7) = 24 (+7) = 31$$

A variation will occur when each number in the sequence is reduced by a number that remains the same for each reduction eg:

24  20  16  xx  8          | Answer = 12 |

2.   22  12  10  35  xx  16  34  23  11          | Answer = 19 |

This is the x – y = z pattern. The format is that there are three numbers in a row. Here the number on the right has to be taken away from the number on the left to find the number in the middle:

$$22 - 12 = 10 \quad 35 - 19 = 16 \quad 34 - 23 = 11$$

Variations on this basic formula occur when the position of the 'xx' is varied, thus altering the numerical calculation, eg:

xx  14  16    27  9  18    32  8  24          | Answer = 30 |

36  12  24    21  7  14    18  10  xx          | Answer = 8 |

3.   2  4  12  xx  240
$\boxed{\text{Answer} = 48}$

Each number is increased by a constantly increasing multiple factor:

$$2 (\times 2) \; = \; 4 (\times 3) \; = \; 12 (\times 4) \; = \; 48 (\times 5) \; = \; 240$$

A variation occurs when each number is divided by a number that constantly decreases, eg:

480  96  xx  8  4
$\boxed{\text{Answer} = 24}$

4.   7  15  23  26  26  23  xx  7
$\boxed{\text{Answer} = 15}$

Mirror pattern: in this sequence the numbers up to 26 are repeated in reverse order:

7  15  23  26  |  26  23  15  7

5.   6230  83   1472  59   3152  xx   9061  97

$\boxed{\text{Answer} = 47}$

In this problem there are two groups of numbers, one of four numbers (abcd) and the other of two numbers (ef). The first two numbers (a + b) are added to find e, and the second two numbers (c + d) are added to find f:

$$(6 + 2)(3 + 0) = 83 \quad (1 + 4)(7 + 2) = 59$$
$$(3 + 1)(5 + 2) = 47$$

6.   108  93  82  71  71  xx  93  108
$\boxed{\text{Answer} = 82}$

Mirror pattern:

108  93  82  71  |  71  82  93  108

7.   5  11  23  47  xx                    Answer = 95

In this sequence the numbers are increased by a constant multiple factor plus 1 (2n + 1). Thus:

5 (× 2 + 1)   =   11 (× 2 + 1)   =   23 (× 2+1)   =
47 (× 2 + 1)   =   95

8.   17  9  16  12  14  15  xx  18  7      Answer = 11

Hop a number sequence. Here there are two sequences:

17  9  16  12  14  15  xx  18  7

with alternate numbers following different rules:

17 ( – 1)   =   16 (– 2)   =   14 (– 3)   =   11; and,

9 (+ 3)   =   12 (+ 3)   =   15 (+ 3)   =   18

9.   9  27  28  xx  85  255              Answer = 84

In this sequential combination, numbers are alternately increased first by multiplying by a constant factor, with the next number in the sequence being found by the addition of a constant number:

9 (× 3)   =   27 (+ 1)   =   28 (× 3)   =   84 (+ 1) =
85 (× 3)   =   255

Variations occur when the alternate numbers in the sequence may be multiplied and subtracted, eg:

9  27  26  78  xx  231                   Answer = 77

or, divided and added, eg:

64  32  36  18  22  xx                    | Answer = 11 |

or, divided and subtracted, eg:

92  46  44  xx  20  10                    | Answer = 22 |

10.  11  9  18  16  32  xx                | Answer = 30 |

This is a variation of 9. Here the sequence is subtraction followed by multiplication:

11 (– 2  =  9 (× 2)  =  18 (– 2)  =  16 (× 2)  =  32 (– 2)  =  30

11.  840  168  xx  14  7                  | Answer = 42 |

840 (divide by 5)  =  168 (divide by 4)  =  42 (divide by 3)  =  14 (divide by 2)  =  7

12.  18  24  28  36  36  28  xx  18       | Answer = 24 |

Mirror pattern:

18  24  28  36 | 36  28  24  18

13.  124  16    592  61    xx3  20    416  47

| Answer = 17 |

The format here is that there is a group of three numbers (abc) and a group of two numbers (de). The first two numbers (ab) in fact make up one double digit number (x) and the third number a single digit number (y). The group of two numbers (de) is one double digit number (z). Thus the basic formula is: $x + y = z$:

$$12 + 4 = 16 \quad 59 + 2 = 61 \quad 17 + 3 = 20$$
$$41 + 6 = 47$$

Variations occur when the 'xx' is placed in a different position thus altering the type of numerical calculation required, eg:

246 xx    328 40    227 29    514 55

| Answer = 30 |

or, when the basic formula is altered so that $x - y = z$, eg,

246 xx    328 24    227 15    514 47

| Answer = 18 |

14. xx  27 26    42 14 28    54 11 43

| Answer = 53 |

Add the middle number to the third number to find the first number:

$$53 = 27 + 26 \quad 42 = 14 + 28 \quad 54 = 11 + 43$$

15. 24 19 15 xx 10

| Answer = 12 |

$$24 (-5) = 19 (-4) = 15 (-3) = 12 (-2) = 10$$

16. 216 54 xx 9

| Answer = 18 |

216 (divided by 4)  =  54 (divided by 3)  =  18
(divided by 2)  =  9

17. 217 14    184 14    417 34    385 xx

| Answer = 33 |

$21 - 7 = 14$    $18 - 4 = 14$    $41 - 7 = 34$
$38 - 5 = 33$

18. 648 72    374 41    622 xx    381 39

Answer = 64

$64 + 8 = 72$    $37 + 4 = 41$    $62 + 2 = 64$
$38 + 1 = 39$

19. 628 54    311 30    627 55    298 xx

Answer = 21

$62 - 8 = 54$    $31 - 1 = 30$    $62 - 7 = 55$
$29 - 8 = 21$

20. 47 22 25    36 14 22    27 15 xx

Answer = 12

Subtract middle number from first number to find third:

$47 - 22 = 25$    $36 - 14 = 22$    $27 - 15 = 12$

21. 3 5 9 17 xx

Answer = 33

$3 (\times 2) - 1 =$    $5 (\times 2) - 1 =$    $9 (\times 2) - 1 =$
$17 (\times 2) - 1 = 33$

An alternative method is:

$3 + = 5 + 4 = 9 + 8 = 17 + 16 = 33.$

22. 4216 67    2531 74    6151 76    6132 xx

Answer = 75

Add first two numbers for tens and second two for units:

$$(4 + 2)(1 + 6) = 67 \quad (2 + 5)(3 + 1) = 74$$
$$(6 + 1)(5 + 1) = 76 \quad (6 + 1)(3 + 2) = 75$$

23. 6 6 8 12 12 24 20 xx 6      Answer = 48

This is an alternate sequence:

6 6 8 12 *12* 24 *20* xx *36*

One sequence is increasing by a factor of 2:

6 12 24 48

The other is increasing at a rate of twice the previous difference:

*6 (+ 2) = 8 (+ 4) = 12 (+ 8) = 20 (+ 16) = 36*

24. 8 17 35 xx 143      Answer = 71

8 (× 2) + 1 = 17 (× 2) + 1 = 35 (× 2) + 1 = 71
(× 2) + 1 = 143

An alternative method is:

8 + = 17 + 18 = 35 + 36 = 71 + 72 = 143

# Visit Kogan Page on-line

Comprehensive information on
Kogan Page titles

**Features include**

- complete catalogue listings,
  including book reviews and
  descriptions

- on-line discounts on a variety
  of titles

- special monthly promotions

- information and discounts on
  NEW titles and BESTSELLING titles

- a secure shopping basket facility
  for on-line ordering

- infoZones, with links and
  information on specific areas of
  interest

PLUS everything you need to know
about KOGAN PAGE

# http://www.kogan-page.co.uk